INTERACTION BETWEEN COMPILERS AND COMPUTER ARCHITECTURES

THE KLUWER INTERNATIONAL SERIES
IN ENGINEERING AND COMPUTER SCIENCE

INTERACTION BETWEEN COMPILERS AND COMPUTER ARCHITECTURES

edited by

Gyungho Lee
Iowa State University
Ames, IA, U.S.A.

Pen-Chung Yew
University of Minnesota
Minneapolis, MN, U.S.A.

KLUWER ACADEMIC PUBLISHERS
Boston / Dordrecht / London

ISBN 978-1-4419-4896-0

Distributors for North, Central and South America:
Kluwer Academic Publishers
101 Philip Drive
Assinippi Park
Norwell, Massachusetts 02061 USA
Telephone (781) 871-6600
Fax (781) 871-6528
E-Mail <kluwer@wkap.com>

Distributors for all other countries:
Kluwer Academic Publishers Group
Distribution Centre
Post Office Box 322
3300 AH Dordrecht, THE NETHERLANDS
Telephone 31 78 6392 392
Fax 31 78 6546 474
E-Mail <services@wkap.nl>

Electronic Services <http://www.wkap.nl>

Library of Congress Cataloging-in-Publication Data

Interaction between compilers and computer architectures / edited by Gyungho Lee, Pen C. Yew.
p.cm. – (The Kluwer international series in engineering and computer science)
Includes bibliographical references and index.

1. Compilers (Computer programs) 2. Computer architecture. I. Lee, Gyungho. II. Yew, Pen-Chung, 1950- III. Series.

QA76.76.C65 I517 2001
005.4'53—dc21

2001029677

Printed on acid-free paper.

Printed in the United States of America

Contents

Preface

Interaction between Compilers and Computer Architectures

Effective compilers will allow more efficient execution of application programs on given computer architectures. On the other hand, well-conceived architectural features can support more effective compiler optimization techniques. Good trade-off considerations between compilers and computer architectures are key to the success of designing highly efficient and effective computer systems. From embedded micro-controllers to large-scale multiprocessor systems, it is important to understand the interaction between compilers and computer architectures.

The Annual Workshop on Interaction between Compilers and Computer Architectures (INTERACT) has been organized to promote new ideas and to present recent developments in compiler techniques and computer architectures that enhance each other's capabilities and performance. This book presents revisions of seven papers presented at the Fifth Workshop on Interaction between Compilers and Computer Architectures (INTERACT-5), which was held in conjunction with the IEEE HPCA-7 at Monterrey, Mexico on January 20, 2001.

The first paper is "EquiMax: A New Formulation of Optimal Register-Sensitive Scheduling with Resources Constraints," by Sid-Ahmed-Ali Touati. It tackles a scheduling problem under registers and resources constraints in a wide-issue processor such as VLIW or superscalar. The scheduling problem is solved via an integer linear programming model with a better asymptotic algorithm complexity.

The paper with the title of "An Efficient Semi-Hierarchical Array Layout" by N. P. Drakenberg, F. Lundervall, and B. Lisper proposes a novel layout scheme for arrays, deviating from many typical linear layout schemes. The proposed layout scheme, a semi-hierarchical scheme, is claimed to provide improved TLB and cache behavior.

The third paper is "Impact of Tile-Size Selection for Skewed Tiling" by Yong-Hong Song and Zhiyuan Li, which attempts to improve array accesses in relaxation codes. To improve data locality in a nested loop, "tiling" is often applied at compile time with "loop skewing." This paper discusses a proper tile size for such a skewed tiling with a consideration of dynamic count of memory load instructions.

The fourth paper is "Improving Software Pipelining by Hiding Memory Latency with Combined Loads and Prefetches" by M. Bedy, S. Carr, S. Onder, and P. Sweeny. This paper presents a scheme of combining a load and a prefetch to avoid potential drawbacks of non-blocking loads and explicit software prefetching when they are utilized separately. The paper shows how the compiler and architecture support to combine a load and a prefetch into one instruction, called a prefetching load, can give a lower register pressure as in software prefetching, and at the same time lower load/store-unit requirements as in non-blocking loads. The scheme also is shown to reduce register pressure significantly.

The paper with the title of "Register Allocation for Embedded System in the Presence of Java Exception" by H.-B. Lee, B.-S. Yang, and S.-M. Moon presents a compromised local variable mapping to reduce memory requirement for just-in-time compilation of Java programs in embedded systems with limited memory. The scheme introduced in the paper allocates a local variable in a "try" block to a fixed location so that a simple implementation with a small overhead can be achieved. This paper demonstrates through experiments with SPECjvm98 on ARM microprocessor that the proposed scheme works with little performance degradation, compared to other more flexible, but memory consuming, mappings.

With VLSI technology progressing toward a more aggressive clock frequency scaling, power consumption and wire-delay over logic delay are becoming very important issues in microprocessor architecture and design. The last two papers in this book address the technology issues.

The paper with the title of "Is Compiling for Performance == Compiling for Power?" by M. Valluri and L. John evaluates how the existing compiler optimizations influence energy consumption and power dissipation of a superscalar processor. Their findings show that optimization techniques that improve performance by increasing the overlap in the program during execution can increase the average power dissipation, while optimizations that improve performance by reducing the number of instructions can be used for energy optimization.

The last paper, "A Technology Scalable Architecture for Fast Clock and High ILP" by K. Sankaralingam, R. Nagarajan, D. Burger, and S. Keckler presents a new technology-aware architecture called Grid processor. The Grid processor is designed with the consideration of the technology constraints on wire and pipelining limits, and is consisted of a two-dimensional grid of ALUs. The compiler is used to detect parallelism and to map instructions to the grid of ALUs. The paper claims that the Grid processor may offer the best of both the VLIW and dynamic superscalar architectures.

The INTERACT Workshop has entered its fifth year. In the past five years, many people have helped to make INTERACT a success. We would like to thank all of them. For this year, the INTERACT-5 program committee members are:
Todd Austin, University of Michigan; Rastislav Bodik, University of Wisconsin; Doug Burger, University of Texas-Austin; Antonio Gonzalez, Universitat Politecnica de Catalunya, Spain; Wei Hsu, University of Minnesota; David Kaeli, Northeastern University; Bill Mangione-Smith, University of California at Los Angeles; and Eric Rotenberg, North Carolina State University.

As can be seen from the papers included in this book, understanding the interaction between compilers and computer architectures is a very important aspect of the computer design. We hope that researchers and practitioners of computer architectures and compilers would find this book worthy of reading, and continue to contribute to the INTERACT Workshop in the coming years.

Gyungho Lee
Iowa State University
Ames, IA 50011
ghlee@iastate.edu

Pen-Chung Yew
University of Minnesota
Minneapolis, MN 55455
yew@cs.umn.edu

Chapter 1

EQUIMAX: A NEW FORMULATION OF OPTIMAL REGISTER-SENSITIVE SCHEDULING FOR ILP PROCESSORS

Sid-Ahmed-Ali Touati
INRIA. Domaine de Voluceau, BP 105. 78153 Le Chesnay cedex, France.
Sid-Ahmed-Ali.Touati@inria.fr

Abstract In this article, we give a new formulation of acyclic scheduling problem under registers and resources constraints in multiple instructions issuing processors (VLIW and superscalar). Given a direct acyclic data dependence graph $G = (V, E)$, the complexity of our integer linear programming model is bounded by $\mathcal{O}(|V|^2)$ variables and $\mathcal{O}(|E| + |V|^2)$ constraints according to a target architecture description. This complexity is better than the complexity of the existing techniques which includes a worst total schedule time factor.

Keywords: optimal scheduling, resources constraints, registers constraints, integer programming

1. Introduction

To sustain the increases in processor performance, current compilers try to take benefit from the instruction level parallelism (ILP) present in current generation processors. Multiple operations are issued in the same clock cycle to increase the throughput of the executed operations per cycle. Completing a computation as soon as possible is a scheduling problem constrained by many factors. The most important ones are the data dependencies, the availability of the hardware features and the registers. The data dependencies define the code semantic and the intrinsic available ILP in the code. The resources constraints limit the number of instructions issued during the same clock cycle because of the lack of free functional units (FU). Also, architectural characteristics of current processors reveal heterogeneous and complex pipelined FUs where an operation can use a group of FUs in different clock cycles during its presence in the pipeline. Finally, since accessing a register has a null latency, we need to keep as many values in the registers as possible.

Unfortunately, theoretical studies on scheduling reveal that integrating resources constraints [3] or registers constraints [5] are two NP-complete problems. The problem of scheduling under both registers and resources constraints becomes a very complex task. General compilers use many heuristics to get an optimized schedule in polynomial time complexity. However, embedded applications or real time systems may need optimal (best) schedule. For this purpose, we need a "good" formulation for the problem. A lot of works have been done using integer linear programming (intLP) models. In our work, we present a new formulation of acyclic scheduling such that the complexity of the model generated is lower than the current ones, like we will explain in the end of this article. Our formulation must reduce the resolution time since we considerably reduce the number of variables and constraints in the generated intLP model.

This article is organized as follows. We first present the model of the targeted processors in Section 2 and the acyclic data dependence graph (DDG) to be scheduled in Section 3: in our study, we assume heterogeneous FUs, more than one register type, and delayed latencies of writing into and reading from registers. The problem of acyclic scheduling is briefly recalled in Section 4. After, we define some intLP modeling techniques in Section 5 to show how we linearize some logical operators (disjunction and equivalence) and how we compute the maximum of a set of integers. We then use these techniques to write our EquiMax (Equivalence-Maximum) intLP formulation in Section 6. We present some achieved work in this field in Section 7 and conclude by our remarks and perspectives in Section 8.

2. Machine Description

An ILP processor [15] takes benefit from the inherent parallelism in the instructions flow and issues multiple operations per clock cycle thanks to the pipelined execution and the presence of multiple functional units (FUs). An operation can be executed on one or more functional units (FU). We model the complex behavior of the execution of the operations on FUs by the reservation tables [16]. We attach to each instruction a reservation table (RT) to describe at which clock cycle a FU is busy due to the execution of this instruction on it. A RT consists

FUs →

time ↓

	issue	ALU	MEM	FP	FPdiv
0	1	1			
1		1	1		
2			1		
3					

(a) $\mathcal{RT}_{fload}$

	issue	ALU	MEM	FP	FPdiv
0	1	1			
1					
2					
3					

(b) $\mathcal{RT}_{iadd}$

Figure 1.1. Reservation Tables

of a two-dimensional table, where the number of lines is the latency of the operation, and the columns consists of the set of FUs. Given a RT of an instruction u, $\mathcal{RT}_u(c, q) = 1$ means that u executes on the FU q during the clock cycle c after its issuing. The number of columns in $\mathcal{RT}$ is bounded by the set of FUs, and the number of lines is bounded by the depth of the pipeline.

The target machine $\mathcal{M}$ is described by the set of its hardware resources, its registers types, and the set of operations which execute on these resources:

1 the set of the registers types in the target architecture is $\mathcal{T}$. For instance, the target architecture of the code in Fig. 1.2 has $\mathcal{T} = \{int, float\}$;

2 the resources of the machine are represented by the couple $(Q, \vec{NQ})$:

- $Q = \{q_1, \ldots, q_M\}$ is the set of the different FUs;
- $\vec{NQ} = [N_{q_1}, \ldots, N_{q_M}]$ where N_q is the number of copies of q.

3 the set of instructions is represented by a couple $(\mathcal{IS}, \vec{\mathcal{RT}})$:

- $\mathcal{IS} = \{u\}$ is the instructions set which can be executed on $\mathcal{M}$;
- $\vec{\mathcal{RT}} = [\mathcal{RT}_{u_1}, \mathcal{RT}_{u_2}, \ldots]$ such that $\mathcal{RT}_u$ designates the RT of the instruction u.

In some architectures (superscalar), the processor cannot issue more than m operations even if the number of FUs is greater than m. To handle this case, we consider a virtual "issue' FU' with m copies, such that all instructions use it once at the issue cycle. Figure. 1.1 gives two examples of RTs.

3. DAG Model

A DAG $G = (V, E, \delta)$ consists of a set of operations V, a set of arcs E, and a delay function δ such that $\delta(e)$ is the latency of the arc e. The arcs set E contains the data dependencies and any other precedence constraints. Each operation u has a latency $lat(u)$. We assume one global sink operation $\perp$ in G which reflects the total schedule time: if there is more than one sink node, we add the virtual node $\perp$ with an arc e from each sink s to $\perp$ with$\delta(e) = lat(s)$. A valid schedule of G is a positive integer function σ which associates to each operation u an issue time $\sigma(u)$. Any acyclic schedule σ of G must ensure that:

$$\forall e = (u, v) \in E: \quad \sigma(v) - \sigma(u) \geq \delta(e)$$

The total schedule time of G is noted $\overline{\sigma} = \sigma(\perp)$.

In this article, we consider that each operation $u \in V$ writes into at most one register of a type $t \in \mathcal{T}$. The operations that define multiple values with different types are accepted in our model iff they do not define more than one value of a certain type. For instance, operations that write into a floating point register and set a condition flag are taken into account in our model. We denotes by u^t the value of
type t defined by the operation u.
We also consider the following sets:

1 $V_{R,t}$ is the set of values of type $t \in \mathcal{T}$. In Fig. 1.2, $V_{R,float} = \{a, b, c, d, g, f, h, j, k\}$;

2 $E_{R,t}$ is the set of flow dependency arcs through a value of type $t \in \mathcal{T}$. For instance $E_{R,int} = \{(g, i), (i, f)\}$. If there is some values not read in the DAG, or are still alive after leaving this DAG, these values have to be kept in registers. We consider then that there is a flow arc from these values to $\perp$ (like the flow arc $(k, \perp) \in E_{R,float}$).

Finally, we consider that reading from and writing into a register may be delayed from the beginning of the schedule time (VLIW case). We define the two delay functions $\delta_{r,t}$ and $\delta_{w,t}$ such that:

$$\begin{aligned}
\delta_{w,t}: \quad & V_{R,t} \to \mathbb{N} \\
& u \mapsto \delta_{w,t}(u) / \ 0 \leq \delta_{w,t}(u) < lat(u) \\
& \text{the write cycle of } u^t \text{ into a register of type } t \text{ is } \sigma(u) + \delta_{w,t}(u) \\
\delta_{r,t}: \quad & V \to \mathbb{N} \\
& u \mapsto \delta_{r,t}(u) / \ 0 \leq \delta_{r,t}(u) \leq \delta_{w,t}(u) < lat(u) \\
& \text{the read cycle of } u^t \text{ from a register of type } t \text{ is } \sigma(u) + \delta_{r,t}(u)
\end{aligned}$$

(a) fload [i1], fR_a
(b) fload [i2], fR_b
(c) fload [i3], fR_c
(d) fmult fR_a, fR_b, fR_d
(e) imultadd fR_a, fR_b, fR_c, iR_e
(g) ftoint fR_c, iR_g
(i) iadd iR_g, 4, iR_i
(f) fmultadd fR_b, iR_i, fR_c, fR_f
(h) fdiv fR_d, iR_e, fR_h
(j) fadd fR_j, 1 , fR_j
(k) fsub fR_k, 1 , fR_k

(1) code before scheduling and register allocation

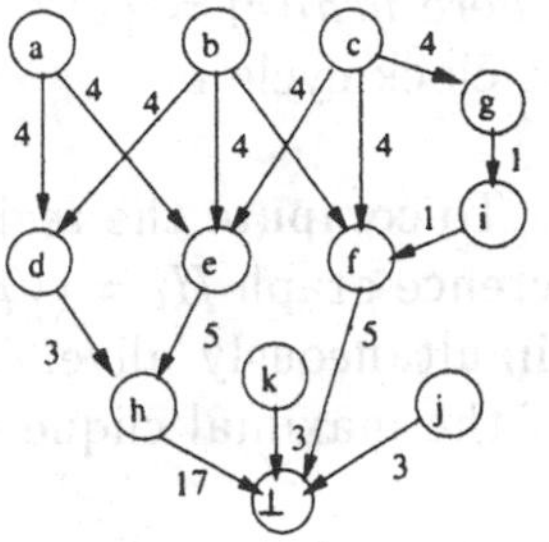

(2) the DDG G

Figure 1.2. DAG model

4. Scheduling Problem

Like explained above, a valid schedule σ of G is first constrained by the inherent data dependency relations between operations or any other serial constraints. The target architecture characteristics impose other constraints which are the limited numbers of registers and resources.

4.1. Registers Constraints

Given a DAG $G = (V, E, \delta)$, a value $u^t \in V_{R,t}$ is alive at the first step after the writing of u^t until its last reading (consumption). The set of consumers of a value $u^t \in V_{R,t}$ is the set of operations that read it :

$$Cons(u^t) = \{v / \exists e = (u, v) \in E_{R,t}\}$$

For instance, $Cons(b^{float}) = \{d, e, f\}$ and $Cons(k^{float}) = \{\perp\}$ in Fig. 1.2. The last consumption of a value is called the killing date and noted ;

$$\forall u^t \in V_{R,t} \quad kill(u^t) = \max_{v \in Cons(u^t)} (\sigma(v) + \delta_{r,t}(v))$$

We assume that a value written at a clock cycle c in a register is available one step later. That is to say, if operation u reads from a register at a clock cycle c while operation v is writing in it at the same clock cycle, u does not get v's result but gets the value that was previously stored in that register. Then, the *lifetime interval* LT_{u^t} of the value u^t is $]\sigma(u) + \delta_{w,t}(u), kill(u^t)]$. Provided the lifetime intervals of all the values, the number of registers of type t needed to store all the defined values is the maximum number of values of type t that are simultaneously alive. We call this number the register need (requirement) and we note it :

$$RN_t(G) = \max_{0 \le c \le \overline{\sigma}} |vsa_t(c)|$$

where $vsa_t(c) = \{u^t \in V_{R,t} / c \in LT_{u^t}\}$ is the set of values of type t alive at clock cycle c.

To compute the register need of type t, we build the indirected interference graph $H_t = (V_{R,t}, \mathcal{E})$, such that u^t and v^t are adjacent iff they are simultaneously alive. The register need $RN_t(G)$ is then the cardinality of the maximal clique (complete subgraph) of H_t.

Since the number $\mathcal{R}_t$ of available registers of type t is limited in the target machine, we need to find a schedule which doesn't need more than $\mathcal{R}_t$ registers for each register type t:

$$\forall t \in \mathcal{T} \qquad RN_t(G) \leq \mathcal{R}_t$$

If we cannot find such schedule, spill code has to be generated, i.e. we must store some values in memory rather than in registers. Spilling increases the total schedule time because it inserts new operations and the spilled data may cause cache misses.

4.2. Resources Constraints

Resources constraints are simply the fact that two operations must not execute simultaneously on the same FU, i.e. the total number of operations which execute on a FU q during a clock cycle c must not exceed the number of the FU copies N_q. By using the reservation tables defined in Section 2, an operation u executes on a FU q during a clock cycle c iff $\mathcal{RT}_u[c - \sigma(u), q] = 1$. Formally, the resources constraints are written:

$$\forall 0 \leq c \leq \overline{\sigma},\ \forall q \in Q \qquad \sum_{u \in V} \mathcal{RT}_u[c - \sigma(u), q] \leq N_q$$

5. Integer Linear Programming Techniques

An intLP problem [8] is to solve:

$$\begin{cases} \text{maximize (or minimize) } cx \\ \text{subject to } Ax = b \end{cases}$$

with $c, x \in \mathbb{N}^n : x \geq 0$, and A is an $(m \times n)$ constraints matrix. This is the standard formulation. In fact, we can use any other linear constraints $(\leq, \geq, <, >, =)$.

5.1. Writing Logical Operators with Linear Constraints

Intrinsically, an intLP problem defines the conjunctive operator $\wedge$: given two constraints matrix A and A', saying that x must be a solution for both $Ax \geq b$ and $A'x \geq b'$ is modeled by :

$$\begin{pmatrix} A \\ A' \end{pmatrix} x \geq \begin{pmatrix} b \\ b' \end{pmatrix}$$

The negation $\neg$ represents a union of solutions spaces rather than an intersection: given a constraints matrix A with m lines (m linear constraints $f_1, f_2, \cdots, f_m$), forcing x to do not verify $Ax \geq b$ is modeled by:

$$f_1(x) < b_1 \ \vee \ f_2(x) < b_2 \ \vee \ \cdots \ \vee \ f_m(x) < b_m$$

In [8], the authors shown how to model the disjunctive operator $\vee$. Consider the problem:

$$\begin{cases} \text{maximize (or minimize) } f(x) \\ \text{subject to : } g(x) \geq 0 \ \vee \ h(x) \geq 0 \end{cases}$$

By introducing a binary variable $\alpha \in \{0, 1\}$, this disjunction is equivalent to:

$$\begin{cases} g(x) \geq \alpha \underline{g} \\ h(x) \geq (1 - \alpha)\underline{h} \end{cases}$$

where $\underline{g}$ and $\underline{h}$ are two known non null finite lower bounds for g and h resp.

We can also generalize to arbitrary number of constraints in a disjunctive formula $\vee_n$:

$$\vee_n(f_1, \cdots, f_n) = (f_1(x) \geq 0 \ \vee \ f_2(x) \geq 0 \vee \cdots \vee \ f_n(x) \geq 0)$$

Since the dichotomy operator $\vee$ is associative, we group the constraints two by two using a binary tree. We can either express $\vee_n$ by grouping the constraints using a perfect binary tree as shown in Fig. 1.3.(a), or using a left associative binary tree as shown in Fig. 1.3.(b). With both techniques, there is $(n-1)$ internal $\vee$ operators [2] which need to define $(n-1)$ boolean variables $(h_1, \cdots, h_{n-1})$. The final constraints system to express $\vee_n$ has $\mathcal{O}(n)$ constraints $(f_1, \cdots, f_n)$ and $\mathcal{O}(n-1)$ boolean binary variables $(h_1, \cdots, h_{n-1})$. The non null lower bounds of the linear functions are always finite. They always can be computed statically and propagated up in the binary tree [17].

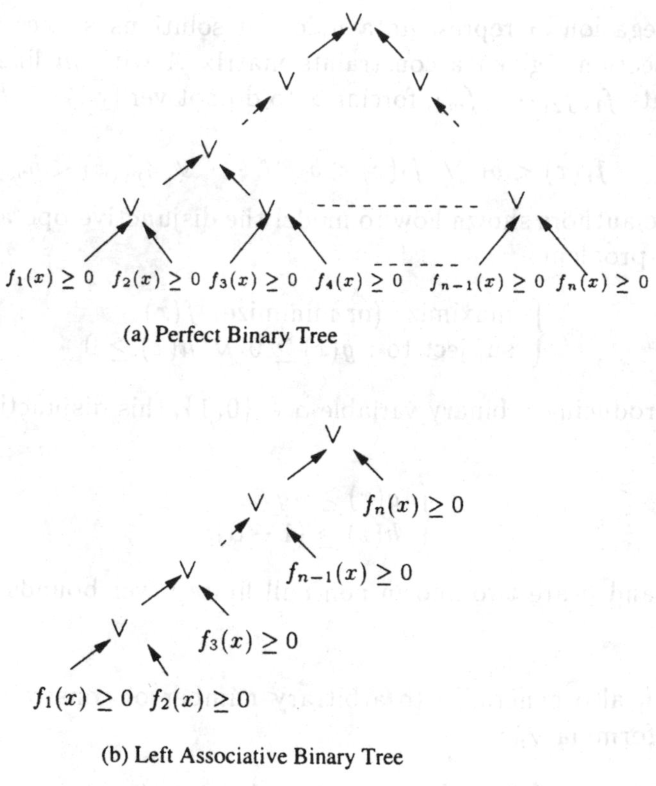

Figure 1.3. Expressing an n-Disjunction with Linear Constraints

From above, we can deduce the linear constraints of any other logical operator:

1 $g(x) \geq 0 \Longrightarrow h(x) \geq 0$ can be written $g(x) < 0 \vee h(x) \geq 0$

2 $g(x) \geq 0 \Longleftrightarrow h(x) \geq 0$ can be written

$$(g(x) \geq 0 \wedge h(x) \geq 0) \vee (h(x) < 0 \wedge g(x) < 0)$$

5.2. Computing the Maximum with Linear Constraints

In our intLP formulation, we need to compute the function $z = max(x, y)$ which can formulated by considering the following constraints:

$$\begin{cases} z \geq x \\ z \geq y \\ z \leq (1-\alpha)x + \alpha\bar{y} \\ z \leq \alpha y + (1-\alpha)\bar{x} \\ \alpha \in \{0,1\} \end{cases}$$

where $(\bar{x}, \bar{y})$ are two finite non null upper bounds for x, y resp. We can also express the max_n function with arbitrary number of parameters $z = max_n(x_1, x_2, \cdots, x_n)$. Since max is associative, we use a binary tree like explained for the n-disjunction operator in Fig. 1.3. The number of internal nodes including the root is equal to $n-1$, so we need to define $n-2$ intermediate variables (that hold intermediate maximums) and $(n-1)$ systems to compute"max" operators. It leads to a complexity of $\mathcal{O}(n-2) = \mathcal{O}(n)$ intermediate variables and $\mathcal{O}(4 \times (n-1)) = \mathcal{O}(n)$ linear constraints (each "max" operator needs 4 linear constraints to be defined) and $\mathcal{O}(n-1) = \mathcal{O}(n)$ binary variables (each max operator needs 1 boolean). The non null upper bounds of the linear functions are always finite if the domain sets of the variables x_i is bounded [17].

6. EquiMax Integer Programming Formulation

In this section, we define a new formulation of scheduling problem using integer linear programming (intLP). We named it EquiMax because it uses the linear constraints which express the equivalence relation ($\Longleftrightarrow$) and the function max_n.

6.1. Scheduling Variables and Objective Function

For all operations $u \in V$, we define the integer variable σ_u that computes the schedule time. The objective function of our model is to minimize the total schedule time i.e. *minimize* $\sigma_\perp$.

The first linear constraints describe the precedence relations, so we write in the model:

$$\forall e = (u, v) \in E \qquad \sigma_v - \sigma_u \geq \delta(e)$$

There is $\mathcal{O}(|V|)$ scheduling variables and $\mathcal{O}(|E|)$ linear constraints. To make the domain set of our variables bounded, we assume T as the worst possible schedule time. We chose T sufficiently large, where for instance $T = \sum_{u \in V} lat(u)$ is a suitable worst total schedule time[1]. Then, we write the following constraint:

$$\sigma_\perp \leq T$$

As consequence, we deduce for any $u \in V$:

- $\sigma_u \geq \underline{\sigma_u} = LonguestPathTo(u)$ is the "as soon as possible" schedule time;
- $\sigma_u \leq \overline{\sigma_u} = T - LonguestPathFrom(u)$ is the "as later as possible" schedule time according to the worst total schedule time T;

6.2. Registers Constraints

6.2.1 Interference Graph. The lifetime interval of a value u^t of type t is

$$LT_{u^t} =]\sigma_u + \delta_{w,t}(u), \max_{v \in Cons(u^t)} (\sigma_v + \delta_{r,t}(v))]$$

We define for each value u^t the variable k_{u^t} that computes its killing date. The number of such defined variables is $\mathcal{O}(|\mathcal{T}| \times |V_{R,t}|)$. Since the domain of our variables is bounded, we know that k_{u^t} is bounded by the two following finite schedule times:

$$\forall t \in \mathcal{T}\ \forall u^t \in V_{R,t} \qquad \underline{k_{u^t}} < k_{u^t} \leq \overline{k_{u^t}}$$

where

- $\underline{k_{u^t}} = \underline{\sigma_u} + \delta_{w,t}(u)$ is the first possible definition date of u^t;
- $\overline{k_{u^t}} = \max_{v \in Cons(u^t)} \left(\overline{\sigma_v} + \delta_{r,t}(v)\right)$ is the latest possible killing date of u^t.

We use the max_n linear constraints to compute k_{u^t} like explained in Section 5.2: we need to define for each k_{u^t} $\mathcal{O}(|Cons(u^t)|)$ variables and

[1]The case where no ILP is exploited.

$\mathcal{O}(4\times|Cons(u^t)|)$ linear constraints to compute it. The total complexity to define all killing dates for all registers types is bounded by $\mathcal{O}(|V|^2)$ variables and $\mathcal{O}(|V|^2)$ constraints.

Now, we can consider H_t the indirected interference graph of G for the register type t. For any couple of values of the same type $u^t, v^t \in V_{R,t}$, we define a binary variable $s^t_{u,v} \in \{0,1\}$ such that it is set to 1 if the two values lifetimes intervals interfere: $\forall t \in \mathcal{T}$, $\forall$ couple $u^t, v^t \in V_{R,t}$

$$s^t_{u,v} = \begin{cases} 1 & \text{if } LT_{u^t} \cap LT_{v^t} \neq \phi \\ 0 & \text{otherwise} \end{cases}$$

For any registers type $t \in \mathcal{T}$, the number of variables $s^t_{u,v}$ is the number of combinations of 2 values among $|V_{R,t}|$ i.e. $\left(|V_{R,t}|\times(|V_{R,t}|-1)\right)/2$.

$LT_{u^t} \cap LT_{v^t} = \phi$ means that one of the two lifetime intervals is "before" the other, i.e. $LT_{u^t} \prec LT_{v^t} \vee LT_{v^t} \prec LT_{u^t}$ where $\prec$ denotes is the precedence operator "before" in the interval algebra [11]. Then, we have to express:

$$s^t_{u,v} = 1 \Longleftrightarrow \neg\left(LT_{u^t} \prec LT_{v^t} \vee LT_{v^t} \prec LT_{u^t}\right)$$

Since $s^t_{u,v} \in \{0,1\}$, these constraints are equivalent to:

$$s^t_{u,v} \geq 1 \Longleftrightarrow \begin{cases} k_{u^t} - \sigma_v - \delta_{w,t}(v) - 1 \geq 0 \\ k_{v^t} - \sigma_u - \delta_{w,t}(u) - 1 \geq 0 \end{cases}$$

Given three logical expressions (P,Q,S), $(P \Longleftrightarrow (Q \wedge S))$ is equivalent to $(P\wedge Q\wedge S)\vee(\neg P\wedge\neg Q)\vee(\neg P\wedge\neg S)$. We write these two disjunctions with linear constraints by introducing two binary variables $h, h' \in \{0,1\}$ (see Section 5) and computing the finite non null lower bounds of the linear functions. This leads to write in the model: $\forall t \in \mathcal{T}$, $\forall$ couple $u^t, v^t \in V_{R,t}$

$$\begin{aligned}
&s^t_{u,v} + h + h' - 1 \geq 0\\
&k_{u^t} - \sigma_v - \delta_{w,t}(v) - min(-1, \underline{k_{u^t}} - \overline{\sigma_v} - \delta_{w,t}(v) - 1) \times (h + h') - 1 \geq 0\\
&k_{v^t} - \sigma_u - \delta_{w,t}(u) - min(-1, \underline{k_{v^t}} - \overline{\sigma_u} - \delta_{w,t}(u) - 1) \times (h + h') - 1 \geq 0
\end{aligned}$$

$$\begin{aligned}
&-s^t_{u,v} - h + h' + 1 \geq 0\\
&-k_u + \sigma_v + \delta_w(v) + min(-1, -\overline{k_{u^t}} + \underline{\sigma_v} + \delta_{w,t}(v)) \times (h - h' - 1) \geq 0
\end{aligned}$$

$$\begin{aligned}
&-s^t_{u,v} - h' + 1 \geq 0\\
&-k_{v^t} + \sigma_u + \delta_w(u) + min(-1, -\overline{k_{v^t}} + \underline{\sigma_u} + \delta_{w,t}(u)) \times (h' - 1) \geq 0\\
&h, h' \in \{0,1\}
\end{aligned}$$

The complexity of computing all the $s^t_{u,v}$ variables is $\mathcal{O}(|V_{R,t}| \times (|V_{R,t}| - 1))$ binary variables (two booleans for each couple of values (u^t, v^t)) and $\mathcal{O}(7/2|V_{R,t}| \times (|V_{R,t}| - 1)|)$ linear constraints (7 linear constraints for each couple of values). The total complexity of considering the interference graph H_t is then bounded by $\mathcal{O}(|V_{R,t}|^2)$ variables and $\mathcal{O}(|V_{R,t}|^2)$ constraints.

6.2.2 Maximal Clique in the Interference Graph.

The maximum number of values of type t simultaneously alive corresponds to a maximal clique in $H_t = (V_{R,t}, \mathcal{E}_t)$, where $(u^t, v^t) \in \mathcal{E}_t$ iff their lifetime intervals interfere ($s^t_{u,v} = 1$). For simplicity, rather to to handle the interference graph itself, we prefer considering its complementary graph $H'_t = (V_{R,t}, \mathcal{E}'_t)$ where $(u^t, v^t) \in \mathcal{E}'_t$ iff their lifetime intervals do *not* interfere ($s^t_{u,v} = 0$). Then, the maximum number of values of type t simultaneously alive corresponds to a maximal independent set[2] in H'_t.

To write the constraints which describe the independent sets (IS), we define a binary variable $x_{u^t} \in \{0, 1\}$ for each value $x_{u^t} \in V_{R,t}$ such that $x_{u^t} = 1$ iff u^t belongs to an IS of H'_t. We must express in the model the following linear constraints:

$$\forall t \in \mathcal{T}\ \forall \text{ couple } x_{u^t}, x_{v^t} \in V_{R,t} \qquad x_{u^t} + x_{v^t} \leq 1 \Longleftrightarrow s^t_{u,v} = 0$$

Since $s^t_{u,v} \in \{0, 1\}$ and by using the linear expressions of the equivalence ($\Longleftrightarrow$), we introduce a boolean $h \in \{0, 1\}$ (see Section 5). The IS are defined in the intLP model by considering:

$$\begin{cases} -x_{u^t} - x_{v^t} + h + 1 \geq 0 \\ -s^t_{u,v} + h \geq 0 \\ x_{u^t} + x_{v^t} - 2h \geq 0 \\ s^t_{u,v} - h \geq 0 \\ h \in \{0, 1\} \end{cases}$$

The number of the variables x_{u^t} is $\mathcal{O}(|V_{R,t}|)$. The number of introduced binary variables to express the equivalences is $\mathcal{O}(1/2 \times |V_{R,t}| \times (|V_{R,t}| - 1))$. The number of linear constraints to define the IS is $\mathcal{O}(2 \times |V_{R,t}| \times (|V_{R,t}| - 1))$.

[2] It is a subgraph such that there is no two adjacent nodes.

The registers constraints are the fact that any set of values simultaneously alive of registers type t must not exceed the number of available registers $\mathcal{R}_t$. The maximal IS in H'_t is the maximal $\sum_{u^t \in V_{R,t}} x_{u^t}$. Thereby, we write in the model ;

$$\forall t \in \mathcal{T} \qquad \sum_{u^t \in V_{R,t}} x_{u^t} \leq \mathcal{R}_t$$

There is $\mathcal{O}(|\mathcal{T}|) = \mathcal{O}(1)$ such constraints. The total complexity of computing the maximal independent sets in H'_t (maximal cliques in H_t) is then bounded by $\mathcal{O}(|V_{R,t}|^2)$ variables and $\mathcal{O}(|V_{R,t}|^2)$ constraints.

6.3. Resources Constraints

6.3.1 Conflicting Graph. The resources constraints are handled by considering for each FU an indirected graph $F_q = (V, \mathcal{E}_q)$ which represents conflicts between the instructions on a FU $q \in \mathcal{Q}$.For any couple of operations, $(u, v) \in \mathcal{E}_q$ iff u and v are in conflicts on q. Any clique in F_q represents the set of operations that use q at the same clock cycle. So, any clique must not exceed N_q the number of the FU copies.

We define a binary variable $f^q_{u,v} \in \{0, 1\}$ such that $f^q_{u,v} = 1$ iff there is a conflict between u, v on the FU q. For each FU, there is $\mathcal{O}(1/2 \times |V| \times (|V| - 1))$ f^q binary variables. To compute them, we use the reservation tables explained in Section 2. Having the RT of two operations types u and v, we can deduce when a structural hazard occurs on a FU q. For example, the operations a and i described in Fig. 1.2 have the RT of Fig. 1.1. These two operations are in conflict on the ALU iff $\sigma_a = \sigma_i \vee \sigma_a + 1 = \sigma_i$. The general formulation of conflicting variables is the disjunction of all cases where a conflict on the FU occurs.

Let $U_{u,q}$ be the set of clock cycles in the reservation table of u where the FU q is used by u:

$$\forall u \in V \ \forall q \in \mathcal{Q} \qquad U_{u,q} = \{c \in \mathbb{N} / \mathcal{RT}_u[c, q] = 1\}$$

The set of all cases where two operations conflicts on a FU q are described by the cartesian product $U_{u,q} \bigotimes U_{v,q}$. The general formula of the binary conflicting variables is then :

$$\forall q \in \mathcal{Q} \ \forall \text{ couple } u, v \quad f^q_{u,v} = 1 \Longleftrightarrow \bigvee_{(c1,c2) \in (U_{u,q} \bigotimes U_{v,q})} \sigma_u + c1 = \sigma_v + c2$$

We use the linear constraints of equivalences and disjunctions defined in Section 5 to write the linear description of this formula in the model. The number of terms in this disjunction depends on $|U_{u,q} \bigotimes U_{v,q}|$ which is a function of the target architecture characteristics (reservation tables and instructions set), and thereby it is a constant for any input DAG. We can write the linear constraints of conflicting cases of all the couples of instructions in $\mathcal{IS}$ only once for the target architecture, and then instantiate them for any input DAG. The total complexity of computing the conflicting variables f^q is bounded by $\mathcal{O}(|V|^2)$ variables and $\mathcal{O}(|V|^2)$ constraints.

6.3.2 Maximal Click in the Conflicting Graph.

For simplicity, rather than considering the conflict graph F_q itself, we use its complementary $F'_q = (V, \mathcal{E}'_q)$ such that $(u, v) \in \mathcal{E}'_q$ iff u and v are *not* in conflicts on q ($f^q_{u,v} = 0$). Then, a clique in F_q becomes an independent set in F'_q.

We define a binary variable $y^q_u \in \{0, 1\}$ for each operation u such that $y^q_u = 1$ iff u belongs to an IS of F'_q. We write in the intLP model the linear constraints of IS :

$$\forall q \in Q \ \forall \text{ couple } u, v \in V \qquad y^q_u + y^q_v \leq 1 \Longleftrightarrow f^q_{u,v} = 0$$

Since $f^q_{u,v} \in \{0, 1\}$ and by using the linear constraints of the equivalence (Section 5), we introduce a binary variable $h \in \{0, 1\}$. These constraints become :

$$\begin{cases} -y^q_u - y^q_v + h + 1 \geq 0 \\ -f^q_{u,v} + h \geq 0 \\ y^q_u + y^q_v - 2h \geq 0 \\ f^q_{u,v} - h \geq 0 \\ h \in \{0, 1\} \end{cases}$$

There is $\mathcal{O}(1/2 \times |V| \times (|V| - 1))$ binary variables h for each FU (one for each couple of operations) and $\mathcal{O}(2 \times |V| \times (|V| - 1))$ linear constraints to describe the IS. The resources constraints are the fact the cardinality of the any independent set in F'_q must not exceed N_q. We write in the model :

$$\forall q \in Q \qquad \sum_{u \in V} y^q_u \leq N_q$$

There is $\mathcal{O}(|Q|) = \mathcal{O}(1)$ such linear constraints.

6.4. Summary

Our integer LP model has a total complexity bounded by $\mathcal{O}(|V|^2)$ variables and $\mathcal{O}(|E| + |V|^2)$ constraints :

1 the objective function : *minimize* $\sigma_\perp$

2 the total number of integer variables is bounded by $\mathcal{O}(|V|^2)$:

(a) $\mathcal{O}(|V|)$ scheduling variables: σ_u for each node $u \in V$;

(b) $\mathcal{O}((|V_{R,t}| \times (|V_{R,t}| - 1))/2)$ interference binary variables for each registers type t: $s^t_{u,v} \in \{0,1\}$ for all couples $u^t, v^t \in V_{R,t}$;

(c) $\mathcal{O}(|V_{R,t}|)$ binary independent sets variables for the complementary interference graph H'_t of the register type t: $x_{u^t} \in \{0,1\}$ for each value $u^t \in V_{R,t}$;

(d) $\mathcal{O}((|V| \times (|V| - 1))/2)$ conflict binary variables for each FU q:
$f^q_{u,v} \in \{0,1\}$ for all couples $u, v \in V$;

(e) $\mathcal{O}(|V|)$ binary independent sets variables for the complementary conflict graph F'_q of each FU q: $y^q_u \in \{0,1\}$ for each operation $u \in V$;

(f) the total number of intermediate and binary variables to write max_n, n-disjunctions and equivalence with linear constraints is bounded by $\mathcal{O}(|V|^2)$;

3 the total number of linear constraints is bounded by $\mathcal{O}(|E| + |V|^2)$:

(a) $\mathcal{O}(|E|)$ scheduling constraints:

$$\forall e = (u,v) \in E \qquad \sigma_v - \sigma_u \geq \delta(e)$$

(b) the total number of interval lifetimes interference constraints is bounded $\mathcal{O}(|V_{R,t}|^2)$ for each register type t:

$$\forall t \in \mathcal{T} \qquad s^t_{u,v} = 1 \Longleftrightarrow \neg(LT_{u^t} \prec L_{v^t} \vee L_{v^t} \prec L_{u^t})$$

(c) the total number of independent sets constraints for the complementary interference graph H'_t is bounded by $\mathcal{O}(|V_{R,t}|^2)$ for each register type t:

$$\forall t \in \mathcal{T} \qquad x_{u^t} + x_{v^t} \leq 1 \Longleftrightarrow s^t_{u,v} = 0$$

(d) the number of registers constraints is $\mathcal{O}(|\mathcal{T}|) = \mathcal{O}(1)$:

$$\forall t \in \mathcal{T} \qquad \sum_{u^t \in V_{R,t}} x_{u^t} \leq \mathcal{R}_t$$

(e) the total number of conflicting constraints is bounded by $\mathcal{O}(|V|^2)$ for each FU q:

$$\forall q \in Q \qquad f^q_{u,v} = 1 \Longleftrightarrow \bigvee_{(c1,c2) \in U_{u,q} \times U_{v,q}} \sigma_u + c1 = \sigma_v + c2$$

(f) the total number of independent sets constraints for the complementary conflict graph F'_q is bounded by $\mathcal{O}(|V|^2)$:

$$\forall q \in Q \qquad y_u + y_v \leq 1 \Longleftrightarrow f_{u,v} = 0$$

(g) the number of resources constraints is $\mathcal{O}(|Q|) = \mathcal{O}(1)$:

$$\forall q \in Q \qquad \sum_{u \in V} y_u \leq N_q$$

(h) the total number of linear constraints to express max_n, n-disjunctions and equivalence is bounded by $\mathcal{O}(|V|^2)$;

We can optimize the length of our model by considering ;

- a precedence constraints $e = (u, v)$ is redundant and can be evicted from the model iff $lp(u, v) > \delta(e)$, where $lp(u, v)$ denotes the longest path from u to v ;

- two values $(u^t, v^t) \in V_{R,t}$ can never be simultaneously alive iff for all the possible schedules one value is always defined after the killing date of the other. This is the case if any of the two following conditions is verified :

$$\begin{array}{ll} \forall v' \in Cons(v^t) & lp(v', u) \geq \delta_r(v') - \delta_w(u) \\ \forall u' \in Cons(u^t) & lp(u', v) \geq \delta_r(u') - \delta_w(v) \end{array}$$

  such that if no path exists between two nodes, we consider it as $-\infty$;

- two operations $u, v \in V$ can never conflict on a FU q iff they can never use q at the same clock cycle. This is the case if any of the two following conditions is verified :

$$\begin{array}{ll} \forall c \in U_{u,q} \ \forall c' \in U_{v,q} & lp(u, v) > c - c' \\ \forall c' \in U_{v,q} \ \forall c \in U_{u,q} & lp(v, u) > c' - c \end{array}$$

  such that if no path exists between two nodes, we consider it as $-\infty$.

7. Related Work

Acyclic scheduling under registers and resources constraints is a classical problem where a lot of works have been done. An intLP formulation (SILP) was defined in [18] to compute an optimal schedule with register allocation under resources constraints. The complexity of this model was bounded by $\mathcal{O}(|V|^2)$ variables and $\mathcal{O}(|V|^2)$ constraints. However, this formulation did not introduce the registers constraints, i.e. it did not limit the number of values simultaneously alive. Moreover, the resources usage patterns which they used was simple and did not formalize the structural hazards that are present in most current ILP processors. A formulation, called OASIC, introduced the registers constraints and was given in [9, 10]. The number of variables was $\mathcal{O}(|V|^2)$ but the number of linear constraints grown exponentially due to the registers constraints. An extension of OASIC formulation was written in [13] to take into account the non regular registers sets (some registers must not be used by some operations) and some other special constraints on ILP which are specific to their target processor characteristics. The registers constraints was formulated but not integrated in the model because of the exponential number of constraints to be generated.

A polynomial formulation for the registers constraints was defined in [5] with a complexity of $\mathcal{O}(T \times |V|)$ variables and $\mathcal{O}(|E| + T \times |V|)$ constraints. Similar approaches minimize the register requirement in exact cyclic scheduling problem (software pipelining) under registers and resources constraints [1, 6, 4]. It is easy to rewrite these intLP models to solve the acyclic scheduling problem. Hanen wrote an original formulation to linearize the disjunctive resources constraints in [12]. The drawback of her formulation was the fact that it treated only simple resources, i.e. an operation can execute only on a single FU. Feautrier in [7] extended this latter to take into account multiple copies of one FU. However, his formulation had the same drawback as [18] and did not treat complex and heterogeneous FUs. The optimal periodic scheduling problem under both registers and heterogeneous resources constraints was formulated in [1, 6, 4]. All these formulations had a complexity which depended on the worst total schedule time T. Indeed, they define a binary variable $\sigma_{u,c}$ for each operation u and for each execution step c during the whole execution interval $[0, T]$. $\sigma_{u,c}$ is set to 1 iff the operation u is scheduled at the clock cycle c. The complexity of their models was clearly bounded by $\mathcal{O}(T \times |V|)$ variables and $\mathcal{O}(|E| + T \times |V|)$ constraints. In fact, the factor T can be very large in real codes since it depends on the input data itself (critical paths and specified operations latencies). We think that a complexity must depend only on the *amount* of input data and not on the date itself. Otherwise, the resolution time would not scale very well. For instance, if we are sure statically that the access to the memory performed by the operation a in Fig. 1.2 is a cache miss, then we would specify that its latency is a memory access (~ 100) rather than a cache access in order to better exploit free slots during scheduling. In this case, the number of variables and constraints in the intLP model is multiplied by a factor of hundred.

The coefficients introduced by our formulation in the final constraints matrix are all bounded by T and $-T$, which is the case of the coefficients in the models defined in [1, 5, 6, 5]. If T is very huge, resolving an EquiMax model or any of the previous formulations may cause computational overflows: in fact, searching for an exact solution of an intLP model needs to compute some determinants of the constraints matrix which can be very huge if the coefficients are sufficiently large [14]. Since EquiMax reduces the size of the constraints matrix, computing these determinants must be less critical with our formulation than with the previous techniques.

8. Conclusion

In this work, we give an intLP formulation of the optimal scheduling under resources and registers constraints. The FUs can have a complex usage pattern and are modeled by reservation tables. We handle the multiple registers types and the delays of the reading from and writing into the registers. The complexity of our model depends only on the number of operations to be scheduled and on the number of serial constraints. Theoretically, our formulation must reduce considerably the time of finding the exact solution. In the future, we will extend our formulation to cyclic scheduling (software pipelining), where the values lifetime intervals and the resources usage patterns become cyclic.

References

[1] Altman, E. (1995). *Optimal Software Pipelining with Functional Units and Registers.* PhD thesis, McGill University, Montreal.

[2] Cormen, T., Leiserson, C. E., and Rivest, R. (1990). *Introduction to Algorithms.* MIT Press, McGraw-Hill, Cambridge, Massachusetts.

[3] Darte, A., Robert, Y., and Vivien, F. (2000). *Scheduling and Automatic Parallelization.* Birkhauser Boston .

[4] Eichenberger, A. E., Davidson, E. S., and Abraham, S. G. (1996). Minimizing Register Requirements of a Modulo Schedule via Optimum Stage Scheduling. *International Journal of Parallel Programming,* 24(2):103–132.

[5] Eisenbeis, C., Gasperoni, F., and Schwiegelshohn, U. (1995). Allocating Registers in Multiple Instruction-Issuing Processors. In *Proceedings of the IFIP WG 10.3 Working Conference on Parallel Archi-*

tectures and Compilation Techniques, PACT'95, pages 290–293. ACM Press.

[6] Eisenbeis, C. and Sawaya, A. (1996). Optimal Loop Parallelization under Register Constraints. In *Sixth Workshop on Compilers for Parallel Computers CPC'96.* , pages 245–259, Aachen - Germany.

[7] Feautrier, P. (1994). Fine-Grain Scheduling under Resource Constraints. In *Proceedings of the 7th International Workshop on Languages and Compilers for Parallel Computing*, Lecture Notes in Computer Science, pages 1–15. Springer-Verlag.

[8] Garfinkel, R. S. and Nemhauser, G. L. (1972). *Integer Programming.* John Wiley & Sons, New York. Series in Decision and Control.

[9] Gebotys, C. H. (1992). Optimal Scheduling and Allocation of Embedded VLSI Chips. In *Proceedings of the 29th Conference on Design Automation*, pages 116–119, Los Alamitos, CA, USA. IEEE Computer Society Press.

[10] Gebotys, C. H. and Elmasry, M. I. (1990). A Global Optimization Approach for Architectural Synthesis. In *Proceedings of the IEEE International Conference on Computer-Aided Design*, pages 258–261, Santa Clara, CA. IEEE Computer Society Press.

[11] Golumbic, M. C. and Shamir, R. (1992). Interval Graphs, Interval Orders and the Consistency of Temporal Events. In *Proceedings of Theory of Computing and Systems (ISTCS'92)*, volume 601 of *LNCS*, pages 32–42, Berlin, Germany. Springer.

[12] Hanen, C. (1990). Study of NP-hard Cyclic Scheduling problem: The periodic recurrent job-shop. In *International Workshop on Compiler for Parallel Computers.* Ecole des Mines de Paris.

[13] Kaestner, D. and Langenbach, M. (1999). Code Optimization by Integer Linear Programming. *Lecture Notes in Computer Science*, 1575:122–136.

[14] Schrijver, A. (1987). *Theory of Linear and Integer Programming.* John Wiley and Sons, New York.

[15] Silc, J., Bobic, B., and Ungerer, T. (1999). *Processor Architecture: from Dataflow to Superscalar and Beyond.* Springer, first edition.

[16] Tokoro, M., Tamura, E., and Takizuka, T. (1981). Optimization of Microprograms. *IEEE Trans. on Computers*, C-30(7):491–504.

[17] Touati, S.-A.-A. (2000). Optimal Register Saturation in Acyclic Superscalar and VLIW Codes. Research Report, INRIA. ftp.inria.fr/INRIA/Projects/a3/touati/optiRS.ps.gz.

[18] Zhang, L. (1996). *SILP: Scheduling and Register Allocation with Integer Linear Programming.* PhD thesis, University of Saarlands.

Chapter 2

AN EFFICIENT SEMI-HIERARCHICAL ARRAY LAYOUT

N.P. Drakenberg*
Department of Teleinformatics, Royal Institute of Technology,
Electrum 204, S-164 40 Kista, SWEDEN
npd@it.kth.se

F. Lundevall
Department of Teleinformatics, Royal Institute of Technology,
Electrum 204, S-164 40 Kista, SWEDEN
f@it.kth.se

B. Lisper
Department of Computer Engineering, Mälardalen University,
P.O.B. 883, S-721 23 Västerås, SWEDEN
bjorn.lisper@mdh.se

Abstract For high-level programming languages, linear array layout have *de facto* been the sole form of mapping array elements to memory, to see widespread use. The increasingly deep and complex memory hierarchies present in current computer systems expose several deficiencies of linear array layouts. One such deficiency is that linear array layouts strongly favor locality in one index dimension of multidimensional arrays. Secondly, the exact mapping of array elements to cache locations depend on the array's size, which effectively renders linear array layouts non-analyzable with respect to cache behavior. We present and evaluate an alternative, semi-hierarchical, array layout which differs from linear array layouts by being neutral with respect to locality in different index dimensions

*Supported in part by the Swedish Research Council for Engineering Sciences (TFR, grant 97-722).

and by enabling accurate and precise analysis of cache behaviors at compile-time.

1. Introduction

Present state-of-the-art compilers do not consistently deliver the performance reasonably expected by users. One of the most fundamental reasons for this is that existing high-level languages invariably induce a perception of memory as being flat, whereas actual computer architectures are being equipped with increasingly deep memory hierarchies to overcome the widening performance gap between processors and main memories.

Devising locality enhanced algorithms, suitable for hierarchical algorithms, is a creative process just as algorithm development in general, and it is therefore not reasonable to expect compilers to automatically derive such algorithms from their non locality-enhanced counterparts. Long-term success in the increasingly important problem of *consistently* obtaining high performance from hierarchical memories will most likely require performance models and languages where locality is somehow exposed. Ideally, this would enable a distinct division of responsibility between compilers and their users, where compilers perform all *architecture specific* tuning, and algorithmic aspects (including algorithmic locality) are managed by humans. For such a division of responsibilities to be meaningful, both parties must be given the means to perform their designated tasks. For a compiler this means, among other things, that logical locality should be reliably translated into effective locality. Consider the following fragment of Fortran 90 code:

```
function mmMpyAdd( A, B, C )
   real, dimension(:,:), intent(in) :: A, B
   real, dimension(:,:), intent(in,out) :: C

   integer L, M, N
   integer i, j, k

   M = size( C, 1 )
   N = size( C, 2 )
   L = size( A, 2 )
   do i = 1, M
      do j = 1, N
         do k = 1, L
            C(i,j) = C(i,j) + A(i,k) * B(k,j)
         end do
      end do
   end do
end function mmMpyAdd
```

In common with most other programming languages, the arrays passed to **mmMpyAdd** as A, B and C are likely to have been dynamically allocated with sizes depending on values input to the program, or being statically non-determinable for other reasons. Having said the above,

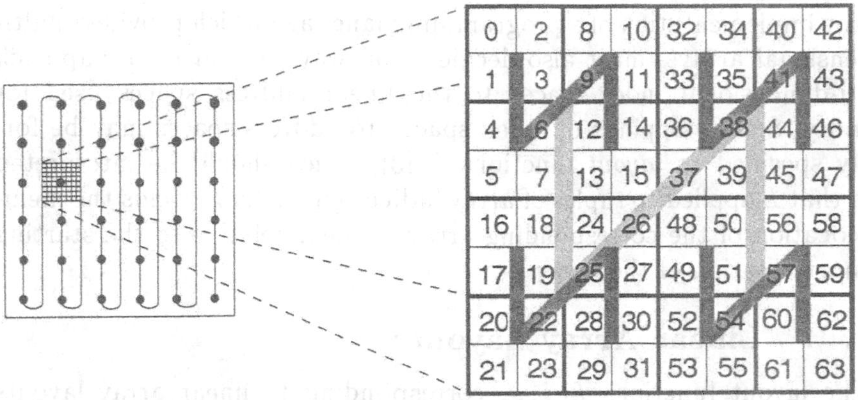

Figure 2.1. The semi-hierarchical array layout (HAT) applied to a two-dimensional array, and using 8-by-8 top-level tiles.

we henceforth assume that array sizes for the most part, cannot be determined at compile time. When using linear array layouts both the direction and distance in the iteration space, between iterations which experience cache interference, depend on the sizes of the arrays involved, and for that very reason cannot be determined at compile time.
We present an alternative, semi-hierarchical, array layout (called HAT) that is shown in Figure 2.1 above, and which addresses the issues raised further above by being effectively dimension-neutral with respect to access distance in memory, and by mapping array elements to memory locations such that the possible cache-location of each element does not depend on the size of the corresponding array.

Our presentation is structured as follows: First, the details of the non-linear semi-hierarchical array layout are presented in Section 2 along with simulation statistics and measured performance results for a (very) small set of computational kernels. Section 3 we show that when using the HAT layout for programs with regular control flow and data references (*i.e.*, nested loops with affine array index expressions), cache conflicts form repeating compact patterns which tessellate the iteration space, and whose exact contents is computable at compile-time. In Section 4 we present related work. Finally, in Section 7, we discuss our results, draw conclusions, and suggest future work.

2. Array Layout

Any implementation of a programming language which provides multi-dimensional arrays, must also decide upon ways in which to map such multi-dimensional index-spaces to the linear address spaces used for memory. Such mappings of index spaces to address spaces may be formally specified as *layout* functions L [3], which should be interpreted such that L applied to tuples of array indices $(i_1, \ldots, i_m)$ yields the memory location of the corresponding array element relative to the starting memory location of the array.

2.1. Linear Array Layouts

The layout functions L_{linear} corresponding to linear array layouts may be expressed as

$$L_{\text{linear}}(i_1, \ldots, i_m) = S_E \cdot \sum_{k=1}^{m} c_k i_k, \tag{2.1}$$

where S_E denotes the size of array elements. The ubiquitous row major and column major orderings are both linear array layouts which simply correspond to different choices of $c_1, \ldots, c_m$. The most significant benefit of row major and column major layouts is due to their linearity (*i.e.*, $L(\alpha\mathbf{i}+\beta\mathbf{j}) = \alpha L(\mathbf{i})+\beta L(\mathbf{j})$), as it enables *incremental* computation of memory addresses for sequences of index tuples. For the very common case of index tuple sequences with a constant difference between successive elements, incremental computation of addresses can be made particularly efficient, and is indeed performed by all modern optimizing compilers.

Sadly, the efficient address computations of linear array layouts are offset by their inclination to interact poorly with hierarchical memory systems when arrays are large. Linear layout functions inevitably map array elements which are adjacent along some direction of the index-space to *consecutive* memory locations, whereas neighboring elements along remaining orthogonal directions tend to occupy widely separated memory locations. Separation of logically adjacent locations makes it unnecessarily difficult for compilers to transform logical locality into effective locality, and in combination with the different behavioral characteristics of caches and TLBs [15] and the influence of array sizes on the mapping of array elements to cache-locations, the task becomes near impossible.

2.2. Hierarchical Array Layouts

An m-dimensional array which is mapped to memory using a *hierarchical layout* can be seen as being recursively constructed from 2^m equally shaped subarrays. Different rules for the relative ordering of the constituent subarrays lead to globally distinct hierarchical array layouts, which are known by names such as C-order, U-order, Hilbert order and Z or Morton order [16] (an example of transposed Morton, or Z^T-layout is provided by the right hand-side of Figure 2.1). Hierarchical array layouts have been developed and used for various special purposes, such as in computational subroutine "libraries" [4, 3], load balancing of parallel computations [12, 17], and in image processing [8, 27].

Despite a non negligeable volume of results on hierarchical storage layouts, such results have typically not become widely known. Several authors seem to have reinvented such storage layouts plus associated concepts and results themselves [D.S. Wise, personal communication], only to subsequently find them scattered among an unusually wide assortment of scientific publications [23, 16, 20]. Our motive for reinventing the Morton order was to enable accurate and precise compile-time analysis of cache behavior and to simplify simultaneous locality enhancement with respect to complete memory hierarchies (*e.g.*, both cache and TLB).

A downside of pure hierarchical array layouts based on globally constant subarray shapes, is that they potentially waste huge amounts of address-space for arrays whose shape deviates from the subarray defining its layout.[1] To avoid this we have chosen to combine a linear layout with a hierarchical layout, by using the hierarchical Morton order for subarrays up to one or several TLB pages in size, and let these subarrays in turn, be ordered according to the linear layout. The resulting *semi-hierarchical* array layout is called HAT (for "Hierarchical Array Tiling").

2.2.1 Address Arithmetic. The computation of addresses from indices does look like a potential source of inefficiency for hierarchical array layouts. Fortunately, for a Morton (and transposed Morton) ordering based on $2 \times \cdots \times 2$ subarrays (as used for HAT), the addresses of array elements are computable from indices through simple bit operations, leading to a definition of the layout function for transposed

[1] Wise has recently pointed out that only address space, not actual storage, is being wasted. His conclusion that such waste is harmless overall will, in our opinion, require more experimental evidence than given in [25].

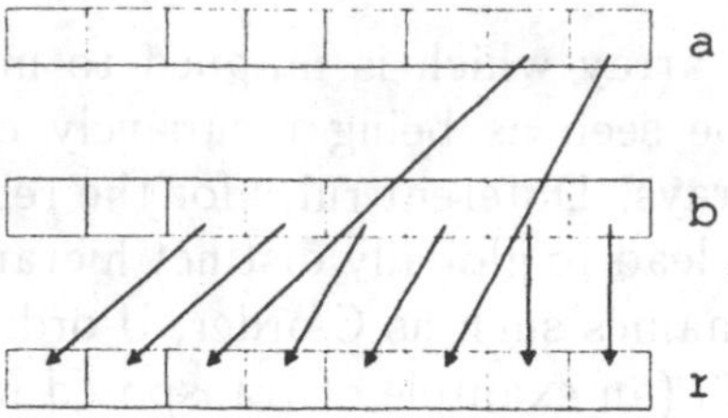

Figure 2.2. An ∇^2 operation, generating an 8-bit result.

Morton order as:

$$L_{\text{Morton}}(i_1, \ldots, i_m) = S_E(i_m \nabla^{m-1}(\cdots(i_2 \nabla^1 i_1)\cdots)) \qquad (2.2)$$

where ∇^k is an operator[2] such that $r = (a \nabla^k b)$ is the interleaving of groups of k bits from b with single bits from a, as shown in Figure 2.2 (next page) for $k = 2$. From (2.2) it is easily seen that the mapping of array elements to memory is *independent of an array's size* and that address computations may be performed through simple bit-operations, but current processor architectures rarely include ∇-operations in their instruction sets, nor are these operations easily synthesized as short sequences of common instructions, and as a consequence direct evaluation of L_{Morton} will be rather expensive. Interestingly, this is not vastly different from linear layouts, for which the integer multiplications in L_{linear} makes its direct evaluation costly. Surprisingly, incremental updating of addresses can be efficiently done also for arrays using Morton order as is demonstrated by the following example:

Example 1 *Consider the index tuple* (3, 5) *of a two dimensional array of single precision floats, whence*

$$L_{Morton}(3,5) = 4 \cdot (3 \nabla^1 5) = 4 \cdot (0000101 \nabla^1 00000011) = 10011100 = 156,$$

which may be decomposed into components corresponding to each index as:

$$10011100 = 00010100 \vee 10001000,$$

[2]The visual appearance of ∇ is intended to suggest the interleaving of bits from two sources.

where $\vee$ denotes the bitwise or of its two operands. Now, given the pair of values or:ed to form $L_{Morton}(3,5)$, we may compute $L_{Morton}(3+3,5)$ as follows:

$$
\begin{array}{rcrcl}
\mathtt{00010100} & & & & \\
\underline{+\,\mathtt{10101000}} & & & & \\
\mathtt{10111100} & & & & \\
\underline{+\,\mathtt{00010100}} & & & & \\
\mathtt{11010000} & & & & \\
\underline{\wedge\,\mathtt{01010100}} & & & & \\
\mathtt{01010000} & \vee & \mathtt{10001000} & & \\
 & = & \mathtt{11011000} & = & 216.
\end{array}
$$

Formal justification of the operations just performed is provided by the algebra of *dilated* integers [23, 20, 25] (p. 53–55, p. 222–226, and p. 779–781, respectively). For the convenience of our readers we now briefly summarize its most salient features from the references just cited.

Definition 1 *Let s be an integer whose binary representation is given by $s = s_r s_{r-1} \ldots s_1 s_0$, $s_i \in \{0,1\}$, using two's complement representation for negative integers. The integer*

$$s_{\nabla^k} = s_r \underbrace{0\cdots0}_{k\ bits} s_{r-1} \underbrace{0\cdots0}_{k\ bits} \ldots s_1 \underbrace{0\cdots0}_{k\ bits} s_0$$

is called a k-dilated *version of s, or simply a dilated version of s for $k = 1$.*

Definition 2 *The transposed Morton-order offset of array element (i,j) is given by $i_{\nabla^1} \vee j_{\nabla^1} \ll 1$, where $x \ll y$ denotes the left-shifting of x by y. Similarly, for an index tuple (i,j,k) the corresponding offset is given by $i_{\nabla^2} \vee (j_{\nabla^2} \ll 1) \vee (k_{\nabla^2} \ll 2)$, and so on for higher dimensional arrays.*

Theorem 1 *Let m and n be two integers and let m_{d^k} and n_{d^k} be their k-dilations, for some k. Then, if m and n are both nonnegative or both negative,*

$$
\begin{array}{rcl}
m = n & \textit{iff} & m_{\nabla^k} = n_{\nabla^k}, \\
m > n & \textit{iff} & m_{\nabla^k} > n_{\nabla^k}.
\end{array}
$$

Theorem 2 *Let $\oplus_k$ and $\ominus_k$ denote the k-dilated addition and subtraction operators, such that $(i_{\nabla^k} \oplus_k j_{\nabla^k}) = (i+j)_{\nabla^k}$ and $(i_{\nabla^k} \ominus_k j_{\nabla^k}) = (i-j)_{\nabla^k}$, respectively. Then*

$$i_{\nabla^k} \oplus_k j_{\nabla^k} = (i_{\nabla^k} + f_{\nabla^k} + j_{\nabla^k}) \wedge m_{\nabla^k}, \tag{2.3}$$

$$i_{\nabla^k} \ominus_k j_{\nabla^k} = (i_{\nabla^k} - j_{\nabla^k}) \wedge m_{\nabla^k}, \tag{2.4}$$

where m_{∇^k} is the k-dilated form of -1 or **111⋯111**, *and f_{∇^k} is the bitwise complement of m_{∇^k}.*

Note that when either of i_{∇^k} or j_{∇^k} are constants a costly run-time k-dilation may instead be done at compile-time, and in addition, either $i_{\nabla^k} + f_{\nabla^k}$ or $f_{\nabla^k} + j_{\nabla^k}$ may be evaluated at compile-time which further reduces the operation count of address computations.

Returning now to the HAT-layout, we see that the layout function of HAT may be written as

$$
\begin{aligned}
&L_{\text{HAT}}(i_1, \ldots, i_m) = \\
&\qquad S_M \cdot L_{\text{linear}}(i_1 \text{ div } T_1, \ldots, i_m \text{ div } T_m) + \\
&\qquad S_E \cdot L_{\text{Morton}}(i_1 \text{ mod } T_1, \ldots, i_m \text{ mod } T_m),
\end{aligned}
$$

where S_M is the size of the largest Morton ordered subarray (*e.g.*, one TLB-page) and $T_1, \ldots, T_m$ are the sizes along each axis of the array of the largest Morton ordered subarray. S_E denotes the size of individual array elements. The algebra of dilated integers may be used to incrementally update addresses within the Morton ordered subarrays of HAT.

2.3. Experimental Evaluation

To evaluate the performance and behavior of the HAT layout, we have rewritten a small set of Fortran kernels to take problem size as a command line argument and to use arrays of corresponding sizes. Compile-time switches are used to select either column major array layout or HAT-layout, where the latter forms have been explicitly devised to incrementally update addresses of array elements by using dilated integers. No other changes have been made to the programs which means that the reported results correspond to the performance of the HAT-layout for row and column traversals of the arrays (*i.e.*, non-tiled code). All programs were compiled using the Sun Workshop 5.0 Fortran compiler using near maximum optimization[3] and were run on Sun Ultra 10 workstations equipped with 333 MHz UltraSPARC-IIi microprocessors, 2Mb of unified 2nd level cache, 640Mb of main memory, which run the Solaris 2.6 operating system. Cache and TLB statistics were obtained using SpixTools/Shade [5] running identical binaries as used for timing measurements, configured to simulate 16Kb direct mapped data and instruction caches and 60-entry fully associative data and instruction TLBs. (Solaris alledgedly locks four TLB entries of each type for kernel use). Reported L1 miss rate statistics were gathered under the assumptions of a perfect data TLB.

[3] -xtarget=ultra2 -xarch=v8plusa -xO5 -depend.

The benchmark codes for which results are shown in Figures 2.3 and 2.4 (GMTRY and VPENTA from the NAS kernel benchmark) were chosen for not exclusively traversing arrays along the most favorable index dimension. These codes were however *not* designed for the HAT-layout. Upon inspection of the diagrams in Figures 2.3 and 2.4, it is immediately visible that the column major layout suffers from very high TLB miss rates whereas the HAT-layout suffers from rather high L1 miss rates. The TLB miss rates experienced by the column major layout is an immediate effect of consecutive accesses not being along the favored index dimension. The HAT-layout is inherently *more* likely to experience high cache miss rates for regular array references, than are linear layouts. However, as we show in the next section, the HAT-layout permits accurate and precise compile-time analysis of its cache behavior, which in turn enables compile-time elimination or reduction of poor cache behavior.

For the HAT-layout, execution time forms a substantially smoother curve than for the column major layout, which by itself might be taken as an indication of easier optimization problems, and distinct bump in execution time for the VPENTA kernel corresponds directly to an increase in L1 miss rates. When comparing execution times, it must also be remembered that for the present experiments, the HAT layout is penalized to a varying degree by the lack of compiler support. The compiler we have used, is completely ignorant of the HAT-layout and therefore does not fully detect common subexpressions or do strength reduction of address computations.

3. Cache Interference & Conflict Vectors

3.1. Cache Interference

The results of this section rely on expressions used in array references being affine functions of loop-control variables from enclosing loops. For such index expressions the mapping of loop-control variables to array indices implied by a reference such as "$\mathsf{A}(\mathsf{I}+1, \mathsf{I}+\mathsf{J}+2)$" may be expressed using matrix notation:

$$\begin{bmatrix} 1 & 0 \\ 1 & 1 \end{bmatrix} \begin{bmatrix} \mathsf{I} \\ \mathsf{J} \end{bmatrix} + \begin{bmatrix} 1 \\ 2 \end{bmatrix}. \tag{2.5}$$

Henceforth, such matrices of coefficients, originating from array references will be called *access matrices* and similarly constant vectors such as $[1\ 2]^T$ in (2.5) are called *offset vectors.*

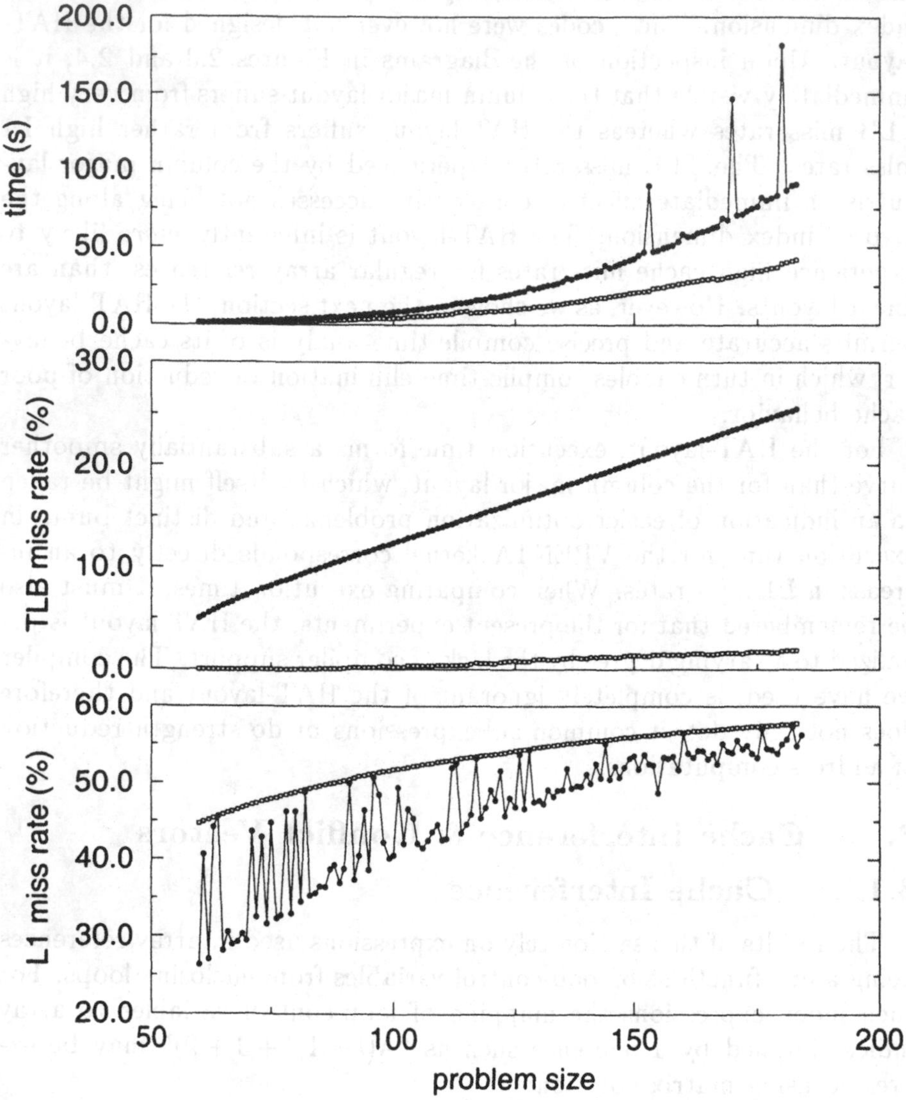

Figure 2.3. Execution time plus cache and TLB miss rates for the NAS GMTRY kernel, *vs* problem size. Filled dots represent column major results, and hollow squares represent HAT-layout results.

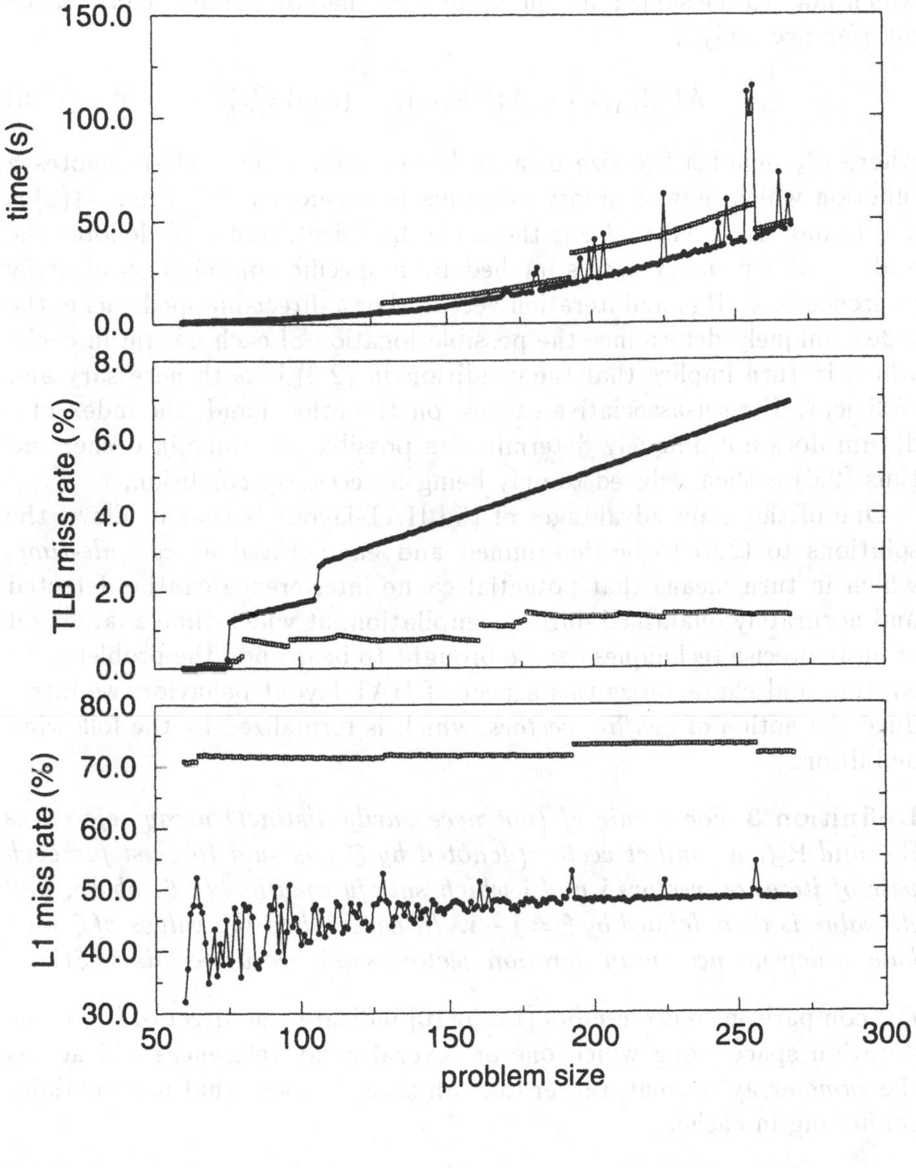

Figure 2.4. Execution time plus cache and TLB miss rates for the NAS VPENTA kernel, *vs* problem size. Filled dots represent column major results, and hollow squares represent HAT-layout results.

3.2. Conflict Vectors

A pair of array references[4] R_A and R_B will access memory locations which map to the same index in cache, and thereby possibly cause cache interference, only if:

$$\mathcal{M}(\langle R_A, \mathbf{i}\rangle) \equiv \mathcal{M}(\langle R_B, \mathbf{j}\rangle) \pmod{C_S}, \tag{2.6}$$

where C_S denotes the size of a cache-set, and where $\mathcal{M}(\cdot)$ denotes a function which maps memory locations to memory-lines[5] (*i.e.*, $\mathcal{M}(a) = a - (a \bmod L_S)$, where L_S is the cache line-size), and $\langle \cdot, \cdot \rangle$ denotes the address of a memory access implied by a specific combination of array reference (*e.g.*, R_A) and iteration vector. For a direct-mapped cache, the index uniquely determines the possible location of each datum in cache which in turn implies that the condition in (2.6) is both necessary and sufficient. For set-associative caches, on the other hand, the index of a datum does not uniquely determine its possible locations in cache, and thus (2.6) is then reduced to only being a necessary condition.

One of the main advantages of the HAT-layout is that it allows the solutions to (2.6) to be determined and enumerated at *compile-time*, which in turn means that potential cache interference can be detected and accurately quantified during compilation, at which time a larger set of more precise techniques can be brought to bear upon the problem. To capture and characterize this aspect of HAT-layout behavior, we introduce the notion of *conflict vectors*, which is formalized by the following definition:

Definition 3 *For a pair of (not necessarily distinct) array references* R_A *and* R_B*, a conflict vector (denoted by* $\boldsymbol{\xi}$[6]*) is said to exist for each pair of iteration vectors* $\mathbf{i}$ *and* $\mathbf{j}$ *which satisfy equation (2.6) above, and its value is then defined by* $\boldsymbol{\xi} = \mathbf{j} - \mathbf{i}$*. In cases when the values of* $\boldsymbol{\xi}$ *may have a dependence on an iteration vector, say* $\mathbf{i}$*, we write this as* $\boldsymbol{\xi}(\mathbf{i})$.

For comparison, *reuse vectors* [14, 9, 10] indicate the direction(s) in the iteration space along which one or several array references will access the *same* array element, rather than an array element that is potentially conflicting in cache.

---

[4]Using the terminology of Ghosh *et al.* [9, 10], we refer to a static read or write in a program as a *reference*, whereas a particular execution of that read or write at runtime is a *memory access*.

[5]A *memory line* refers to a cache line sized-and-aligned block in memory, while a *cache line* refers to the actual block in cache to which a memory line is mapped.

[6]The greek symbol ξ was chosen because of the acronym-like correspondence: ξ = xi ≈ *abbrev.* cross interference.

3.3. Computing Conflict Vectors

The mapping of array indices to memory locations, as well as efficient address computations, for arrays that use the HAT-layout have been described in the previous section. However, for the purpose of computing conflict vectors it is more convenient to work with the reverse mapping, from storage locations to array indices. The mapping from storage locations, $\mathbf{s}$, to array indices, $\mathbf{i}$, implied by the Morton order for an m-dimensional array may be expressed as the matrix-vector product:

$$\mathbf{i} = \begin{bmatrix} \mathbf{I}_m & 2\mathbf{I}_m & 4\mathbf{I}_m & 8\mathbf{I}_m & \cdots \end{bmatrix} \mathbf{s}, \qquad (2.7)$$

where $\mathbf{I}_m$ is the identity matrix of order m, and where the vector $\mathbf{s}$ is the *binary* encoding of the storage location. As an example, consider the case of a two-dimensional array; the mapping of storage locations to array indices implied by (2.7) is then given by

$$\mathbf{i} = \begin{bmatrix} 1 & 0 & 2 & 0 & 4 & 0 & 8 & 0 & \cdots \\ 0 & 1 & 0 & 2 & 0 & 4 & 0 & 8 & \cdots \end{bmatrix} \mathbf{s},$$

and it is easily seen how the different components of $\mathbf{i}$ are formed from even and odd components (bits) of the storage location. In the case of a three-dimensional array, the components of $\mathbf{i}$ would be formed from every third component (bit) of $\mathbf{s}$, and so on. Naturally, mappings of storage locations to array indices have a fundamental role in the computation of conflict vectors, and for this reason, $\mathbf{H}_m^c$ where 2^c is the size of Morton ordered subarrays, is consistently used to denote the matrix $[\mathbf{I}_m\, 2\mathbf{I}_m\, 4\mathbf{I}_m \cdots 2^{c-1}\mathbf{I}_m]$ throughout the rest of this text.

In section 2 it is shown how, after reaching a predefined and carefully chosen size-limit, the HAT-layout changes from using Morton order to using column major order. As a consequence, the mapping of storage locations to array indices given in (2.7) is incomplete and needs to be augmented with a linear term corresponding to the transition to a linear layout. Doing so, and simultaneously replacing the left hand-side of equation (2.7) with the mapping from iteration space to index space implied by some reference, say R_B, yields an expression for the correspondence between iteration space coordinates and storage locations for that array reference:

$$\mathbf{B}\mathbf{j} + \mathbf{b} = \mathbf{H}_{d_B}^c \mathbf{s} + \mathbf{L}_{d_B}^c \mathbf{q}. \qquad (2.8)$$

In (2.8), $\mathbf{j}$ is an iteration vector, $\mathbf{B}$ and $\mathbf{b}$ are the access matrix and offset vector respectively of reference R_B and d_B denotes the dimensionality of array accessed through reference R_B. The meaning of $\mathbf{H}_{d_B}^c$ is given above and $\mathbf{L}^c_{d_B}$ is a diagonal matrix with elements identical to the sizes of Morton ordered subarrays along corresponding dimensions. As an example, given Morton ordered regions of 8192 bytes ($c = 10$), and an array reference $\mathsf{B}(\mathsf{I}+1, \mathsf{I}+\mathsf{J}+2)$ where B is a two-dimensional array of eight-byte elements, the corresponding instance of (2.8) is:

$$\begin{bmatrix} 1 & 0 \\ 1 & 1 \end{bmatrix}\mathbf{j} + \begin{bmatrix} 1 \\ 2 \end{bmatrix} = \begin{bmatrix} 1 & 0 & 2 & 0 & 4 & 0 & 8 & 0 & 16 & 0 \\ 0 & 1 & 0 & 2 & 0 & 4 & 0 & 8 & 0 & 16 \end{bmatrix}\mathbf{s} + \begin{bmatrix} 32 & 0 \\ 0 & 32 \end{bmatrix}\mathbf{q},$$

where $\mathbf{j} \in \mathbb{Z}^2$, $\mathbf{s} \in \{0,1\}^{10}$, and $\mathbf{q} \in \mathbb{Z}^2$.

As indicated in section 2 it is wise to chose transition points between linear and non-linear layouts such that an integer multiple (≥ 1) of Morton ordered regions fit and are aligned in each cache-set. The usefulness of such a choice is due to the modulo-C_S indexing of typical caches, which causes the values of $\mathbf{q}$-vectors in (2.8) to become largely unrelated to the cache behavior of reference R_B. The binary vector $\mathbf{s}$ in (2.8) indicates the offset of an array element in some Morton-ordered region. Since the size and alignment of Morton ordered regions is tailored to the cache parameters, and assuming temporarily that all array elements and cache lines are of equal size (how to remove this restriction is discussed on pages 14 and 16), the values of $\mathbf{s}$ for any pair of conflicting accesses must be equal. Thereafter, and if keeping equation (2.8) in memory, it is easily realized that any conflict vector $\boldsymbol{\xi}(\mathbf{j})$ of reference R_B w.r.t. R_A must satisfy

$$\begin{aligned} \mathbf{A}(\mathbf{j}+\boldsymbol{\xi}) + \mathbf{a} &= \mathbf{H}^c_{d_A}\mathbf{s} + \mathbf{L}^c_{d_A}\mathbf{p} \\ \mathbf{B}\mathbf{j} + \mathbf{b} &= \mathbf{H}^c_{d_B}\mathbf{s} + \mathbf{L}^c_{d_B}\mathbf{q}, \end{aligned} \tag{2.9}$$

where $\mathbf{s} \in \{0,1\}^c$, $\mathbf{p} \in \mathbb{Z}^{d_A}$, $\mathbf{q} \in \mathbb{Z}^{d_B}$, and where $\mathbf{A}, \mathbf{B}$ and $\mathbf{a}, \mathbf{b}$ are the access matrices and offset vectors of references R_A and R_B respectively.

Cache interference phenomena are conventionally categorized as being due either to *self-interference* or *cross-interference* [14]. Self-interference represents the case when it is memory accesses of the same reference that interfere in cache, and cross-interference represents all other cases of interference. To simplify the presentation, and to remain "compatible" with existing literature, the computation of conflict vectors is described separately for self-interference and for cross-interference.

3.4. Self Interference

When references R_A and R_B are not distinct, we have $\mathbf{A} = \mathbf{B}$ and $\mathbf{a} = \mathbf{b}$, and of course $d_A = d_B$ in equation (2.9), which may then (because of $\mathbf{H}^c_{d_A} = \mathbf{H}^c_{d_B}$) be rewritten as:

$$\mathbf{B}\boldsymbol{\xi} + \mathbf{Bj} + \mathbf{b} - \mathbf{L}^c_{d_B}\mathbf{p} = \mathbf{Bj} + \mathbf{b} - \mathbf{L}^c_{d_B}\mathbf{q},$$

which in turn is easily reduced to

$$\mathbf{B}\boldsymbol{\xi} - \mathbf{L}^c_{d_B}\mathbf{r} = \mathbf{0}, \tag{2.10}$$

where $\mathbf{r} = (\mathbf{p} - \mathbf{q}) \in \mathbb{Z}^{d_B}$. Equation (2.10) is a system of linear Diophantine equations, and as such it may be solved by any one of the existing methods for solving such systems of equations, see for example, [21] (p. 52–59) or [26] (p. 106–117). By the theorem below, the set of integer solutions to (2.10) can be represented by a set of linearly independent integer vectors:

Theorem 3 *For any matrix* $\mathbf{A} \in \mathbb{Q}^{m \times n}$ *and vector* $\mathbf{b} \in \mathbb{Q}^m$ *such that* $\mathbf{A}\mathbf{x}_0 = \mathbf{b}$ *for* $\mathbf{x}_0 \in \mathbb{Z}^n$, *a set of integral vectors* $\mathbf{x}_0, \mathbf{x}_1, \ldots, \mathbf{x}_t$, *exist, such that*

$$\{\mathbf{x}|\mathbf{A}\mathbf{x} = \mathbf{b}, \mathbf{x} \in \mathbb{Z}^n\} = \{\mathbf{x}_0 + \lambda_1\mathbf{x}_1, \ldots, \lambda_t\mathbf{x}_t | \lambda_1, \ldots, \lambda_t \in \mathbb{Z}\}, \tag{2.11}$$

where $\mathbf{x}_1, \ldots, \mathbf{x}_t$ *are linearly independent, and* $t = n - \text{rank}(\mathbf{A})$.
Proof: *See Corollary 4.1c in [21] (p. 45–48).*

Note that solutions to (2.10) where $\boldsymbol{\xi}$ belongs to the nullspace or kernel of $\mathbf{B}$ (*i.e.*, $\boldsymbol{\xi} \in \{\boldsymbol{\alpha}|\mathbf{B}\boldsymbol{\alpha} = \mathbf{0}\}$, commonly denoted by $\boldsymbol{\xi} \in \text{null}(\mathbf{B})$ or $\boldsymbol{\xi} \in \ker(\mathbf{B})$) represent temporal reuse rather than potentially conflicting accesses. The components of solution vectors corresponding to $\mathbf{r}$ lets us distinguish between reuse and conflict without computing the nullspace of $\mathbf{B}$. Any solution representing a potential conflict must have some non-zero $\mathbf{r}$-component, since otherwise the pair of accesses are in fact accessing the same location which by definition is a case of reuse. Thus, the set of self-conflict vectors is chosen as the $\boldsymbol{\xi}$-components of the basis indicated by Theorem 3, for which the $\mathbf{r}$-components are non-zero. For multi-word cache-lines, potential conflicts exist that do not satisfy (2.10). An augmented set of self-conflict vectors corresponding to multi word cache lines of some known constant length can be obtained by solving variants of (2.10) with different right hand sides corresponding to how the Morton order in question maps array elements to cache lines. Doing so yields sets of slightly different conflict vectors for adjacent iterations, which may be more conveniently and compactly represented by the union of all such sets, albeit at the loss of some precision.

Under the assumption that base-addresses of multidimensional arrays that use the HAT-layout are aligned on cache-set boundaries, an identical derivation of conflict vectors applies also to references which access different arrays, but which use otherwise identical access expressions. However, in the latter case, solutions for which $\boldsymbol{\xi} \in \ker(\mathbf{B})$, including $\boldsymbol{\xi} = \mathbf{0}$ *do* represent true conflicts. Alternatively, assume the same constraints as immediately above, with the exception that arrays using the HAT layout are *not* constrained to cache-set boundaries, but that the relative alignment of such arrays is somehow known. Then the expression corresponding to equation (2.10) will (typically) have a non-null right hand-side, corresponding to the difference in alignment of the arrays.

3.5. Cross Interference

For a pair of distinct references R_A and R_B, possibly to arrays of differing dimensionalities, (2.9) can not be simplified in the manner done for self-interference above. Furthermore, cross-interference behavior is inherently more varied and more complex to characterize. By trying to solve (2.9) directly, the regularity and structure which exist among solutions easily becomes obscured. Instead it is useful to study a "reduced" system of equations, corresponding to the iterations $\mathbf{j}'$ such that the references R_A and R_B without offset vectors, would access conflicting locations:

$$\begin{aligned} \mathbf{A}\mathbf{j}' &= \mathbf{H}^c_{d_A}\mathbf{s}' + \mathbf{L}^c_{d_A}\mathbf{p}' \\ \mathbf{B}\mathbf{j}' &= \mathbf{H}^c_{d_B}\mathbf{s}' + \mathbf{L}^c_{d_B}\mathbf{q}', \end{aligned} \tag{2.12}$$

where $\mathbf{s}' \in \{0,1\}^c$, $\mathbf{p}' \in \mathbb{Z}^{d_A}$, $\mathbf{q}' \in \mathbb{Z}^{d_B}$, and where $\mathbf{A}$ and $\mathbf{B}$ are the access matrices of references R_A and R_B, respectively, and $\mathbf{j}'$ is an iteration vector. The significance of (2.12) is that for any pair of solutions $\{(\mathbf{j},\mathbf{s},\mathbf{p},\mathbf{q}),(\mathbf{j}',\mathbf{s}',\mathbf{p}',\mathbf{q}')\}$ to (2.9) and (2.12) such that $\mathbf{s}^{\mathrm{T}} \cdot \mathbf{s}' = 0$, we clearly have $\boldsymbol{\xi}(\mathbf{j}) = \boldsymbol{\xi}(\mathbf{j}+\mathbf{j}')$ since $\boldsymbol{\xi}(\mathbf{j}') = \mathbf{0}$, thus specifying *translational symmetry* in the solutions to (2.9). As shown below, the sets of $\mathbf{j}'$ satisfying (2.12) are easily obtained for typical index expressions. Space limitation prevent us from including proofs, which may instead be found in Chapter 6 of [7].

To establish the results just stated, we begin with definitions which distinguish between types of $\mathbf{s}'$-vectors satisfying (2.12), which motivates us to rephrase (2.12) slightly, and label equation instances corresponding to different dimensionalities of $\mathbf{s}'$:

$$\begin{aligned} \mathcal{S}_c = \{\mathbf{s}' \in \{0,1\}^c \mid \exists \mathbf{j}', \mathbf{p}', \mathbf{q}': \\ \mathbf{H}^c_{d_A}\mathbf{s}' = \mathbf{A}\mathbf{j}' - \mathbf{L}^c_{d_A}\mathbf{p}' \wedge \mathbf{H}^c_{d_B}\mathbf{s}' = \mathbf{B}\mathbf{j}' - \mathbf{L}^c_{d_B}\mathbf{q}'\}. \end{aligned} \qquad (2.13)$$

Definition 4 *A vector* $\mathbf{s}' \in \mathcal{S}_c$ *is said to be* reducible *(in* $\mathcal{S}_c$*) whenever* $\mathbf{s}' = \mathbf{s}'_1 + \mathbf{s}'_2$, $\mathbf{s}'_1, \mathbf{s}'_2 \in \mathcal{S}_c$ *and* $\mathbf{s}'_1 \neq \mathbf{0}$, $\mathbf{s}'_2 \neq \mathbf{0}$. *Vectors* $\mathbf{s}' \in \mathcal{S}_c$ *which are not reducible are said to* irreducible, *among which the nullvector,* $\mathbf{0}$, *of appropriate dimensionality is always present due to it being a trivial solution to (2.12).*

Theorem 4 *For any pair of array references* R_A, R_B *such that* $\mathbf{A}$ *and* $\mathbf{B}$ *have elements constrained to the set* $\{-1, 0, 1\}$, *the set of binary vectors* $\mathcal{S}_c$ *is generated by a unique subset of* $\mathcal{S}_c$ *consisting only of irreducible vectors.*

First, each irreducible element of $\mathcal{S}_c$ corresponds to an irreducible element of $\mathcal{S}_{c-1}$. Thus, given the set of irreducible elements of $\mathcal{S}_{c-1}$, the irreducible elements of $\mathcal{S}_c$ may be found by extending each irreducible element $\mathbf{s} \in \mathcal{S}_{c-1}$ (beginning with $\mathbf{s} = \mathbf{0}$) to $[\mathbf{s}^{\mathrm{T}} 1]^{\mathrm{T}}$ and testing for membership in $\mathcal{S}_c$.

Having obtained a complete set of irreducible $\mathbf{s}' \in \mathcal{S}_c$, we may solve (2.12) for each such $\mathbf{s}'$:

$$\begin{bmatrix} \mathbf{A} & \mathbf{L}^c_{d_A} & 0 \\ \mathbf{B} & 0 & \mathbf{L}^c_{d_B} \end{bmatrix} \begin{bmatrix} \mathbf{j}' \\ \mathbf{p}' \\ \mathbf{q}' \end{bmatrix} = \begin{bmatrix} \mathbf{H}^c_{d_A} \\ \mathbf{H}^c_{d_B} \end{bmatrix} \mathbf{s}',$$

using standard methods [21, 26]. By doing so, a set of solutions for $\mathbf{j}'$, on the form $\mathbf{j}' = \{\mathbf{u} \mid \mathbf{u} = \mathbf{v}_0 + \lambda_1\mathbf{v}_1 + \cdots + \lambda_k\mathbf{v}_k\}$, is determined for each irreducible $\mathbf{s}'$, where in turn, $\boldsymbol{\xi}(\mathbf{j}) = \boldsymbol{\xi}(\mathbf{j}+\mathbf{j}')$ for each $\mathbf{j}$ such that $\mathbf{s}^{\mathrm{T}}\mathbf{s}' = 0$, where $\mathbf{s}$ is the location corresponding to $\mathbf{j}$. Note that when the conditions of theorem 4 are not satisfied by a pair of references, the members $\mathbf{s}'$ of $\mathcal{S}_c$ may be determined by enumeration of all elements in $\{0,1\}^c$ and attempting to solve (2.12) for each such $\mathbf{s}' \in \{0,1\}^c$. Typically, however, the elements in access matrices of multi-dimensional arrays are small, giving theorem 4 wide applicability in practice.

Finally a full cross-interference characterization may be determined as the solution to (2.9) for each $\mathbf{s} \notin \mathcal{S}_c$, which minimizes $\|\boldsymbol{\xi}\|_1$. The cross-interference behavior of the pair of references is then perfectly described for each location s, by its conflict vector ξ and the sets of iteration vectors obtained by solving (2.12) for each irreducible $\mathbf{s}' \in \mathcal{S}_c$. Note that for cross conflicts between arrays of equal dimensionality and equal-size elements, storage locations are sufficiently well identified by their corresponding array indices, and thus (2.9) may be simplified to

$$\begin{aligned} \mathbf{A}(\mathbf{j}+\xi)+\mathbf{a} &= \mathbf{l}+\mathbf{L}^c_{d_A}\mathbf{p} \\ \mathbf{B}\mathbf{j}+\mathbf{b} &= \mathbf{l}+\mathbf{L}^c_{d_B}\mathbf{q}, \end{aligned} \qquad (2.14)$$

in such cases.

For multi-word cache lines, an augmented set of conflict vectors is obtained by solving several instances of (2.9) wherein $\mathbf{H}^c_{d_A}\mathbf{S}_1$ and $\mathbf{H}^c_{d_B}\mathbf{s}_2$ are used instead of $\mathbf{H}^c_{d_A}\mathbf{s}$ and $\mathbf{H}^c_{d_B}\mathbf{s}$, respectively, with $\mathbf{s}_1$ $\mathbf{s}_2$ being different locations belonging to same cache line [7].

3.6. Examples

The following program fragment originates from the SPEC95 TOMCATV-benchmark:

```
DO J = 3, N-1
   DO I = 2, N-1
      R = AA(I,J) * D(I,J-1)
      D(I,J) = 1.0/(DD(I,J) - AA(I,J-1)*R)
      RX(I,J) = RX(I,J) - RX(I,J-1)*R
      RY(I,J) = RY(I,J) - RY(I,J-1)*R
   END DO
END DO
```

wherein all arrays (AA, D, DD, RX, RY) have double precision elements. Since the access matrices are identical for all array references above and all arrays are two-dimensional with double precision elements, the matrices $\mathbf{B}$ and $\mathbf{L}^c_{d_B}$ in (2.10) are identical for all array references leading to identical self-interference ξ-vectors. For values of $\mathbf{B}$ and $\mathbf{L}^c_{d_B}$ given by

$$\mathbf{B} = \begin{bmatrix} 1 & 0 \\ 0 & 1 \end{bmatrix} \text{ and } \mathbf{L}^c_{d_B} = \begin{bmatrix} 64 & 0 \\ 0 & 32 \end{bmatrix},$$

corresponding to the access matrices of the references above, and a cache set-size of 16Kb ($c = 14$), the corresponding set of self-interference ξ-vectors, as determined by solving (2.10)

$$\left\{ \begin{bmatrix} 64 \\ 0 \end{bmatrix}, \begin{bmatrix} 0 \\ 32 \end{bmatrix} \right\}$$

as expected. The set of ξ-vectors between references to distinct arrays that use identical index expressions becomes

$$\left\{ \begin{bmatrix} 64 \\ 0 \end{bmatrix}, \begin{bmatrix} 0 \\ 32 \end{bmatrix}, \begin{bmatrix} 0 \\ 0 \end{bmatrix} \right\}$$

and the set of cross-interference ξ-vectors for pairs of the two distinct index expressions present in the program fragment above is obtained by solving (2.14), which yields ξ-vectors

$$\xi = \begin{bmatrix} 0 \\ 1 \end{bmatrix} \text{ and } \xi = \begin{bmatrix} 0 \\ -1 \end{bmatrix}$$

respectively.

As our second example of ξ-vector computation, we consider the following program fragment (from the NAS GMTRY kernel) which performs gaussian elimination:

```
DO I=1,MATDIM
  RMATRX(I,I) = 1.0/RMATRX(I,I)
  DO J=I+1, MATDIM
    RMATRX(J,I) = RMATRX(J,I) * RMATRX(I,I)
    DO K=I+1, MATDIM
      RMATRX(J,K) = RMATRX(J,K) - RMATRX(J,I) * RMATRX(I,K)
    END DO
  END DO
END DO
```

As in the previous example, all arrays are two-dimensional and have double precision elements so that a simpler form of (2.12) derivable from (2.14) may be used for computing cross-interference. For the pair of references MATRX(J,I), MATRX(I,K), the linear system to solve becomes

$$\begin{bmatrix} 1 & 0 & 0 & -64 & 0 & 0 & 0 \\ 0 & 0 & 1 & 0 & -32 & 0 & 0 \\ 0 & 1 & 0 & 0 & 0 & -64 & 0 \\ 1 & 0 & 0 & 0 & 0 & 0 & -32 \end{bmatrix} \begin{bmatrix} i \\ j \\ k \\ p_1 \\ p_2 \\ q_1 \\ q_2 \end{bmatrix} - \begin{bmatrix} u \\ v \\ u \\ v \end{bmatrix} = \begin{bmatrix} 0 \\ 0 \\ 0 \\ 0 \end{bmatrix},$$

for which one finds that

$$\begin{bmatrix} i \\ j \\ k \end{bmatrix} = \lambda_1 \begin{bmatrix} 1 \\ 1 \\ 1 \end{bmatrix} + \lambda_2 \begin{bmatrix} 64 \\ 0 \\ 64 \end{bmatrix} + \lambda_3 \begin{bmatrix} 0 \\ 0 \\ 32 \end{bmatrix}$$

gives the translational symmetry of the complete set of solutions. Enumerating all individual solutions here would clearly require too much space and is easily obtained by scanning the region given above. Hence we conclude our examples by saying that the process is repeated for each distinct pair of references in a loop nest in order to obtain complete information on the cache behavior.

4. Related Work

Array layout has received much attention in the context of automatic array alignment and distribution for distributed memory machines [2, 11, 13]. In the context of uni-processor memory hierarchies, the work of Chatterjee *et al.* [3, 4] is the most similar to ours. They investigate and evaluate an array layout which is essentially identical to the HAT-layout, but which uses a set of smallest tile-sizes within which linear layouts. Significant performance gains are reported for some hand-tailored tiled algorithms using their layout. The basic properties of Morton ordering have been provided multiple times in the literature, the most recent such report being that of Wise [25].

With respect to program analysis, our work is most closely related to the Cache Miss Equations [9, 10]. The cache miss equations (CME) framework, developed by Ghosh *et al.*, identify cache-misses as integer solutions to specific equations. The CME solution count could possibly be used to select between a limited number of transformations, but it is costly to compute even though faster, approximative methods have recently been suggested [24]. Furthermore, unknown array bounds turn up in the equations and counting the solutions would then imply solving the CME symbolically which seems prohibitively difficult. This, however, is not a fault of the CME-framework, but a direct consequence of linear array layouts.

Lam *el al.* point out the destructive effects of self-interference for tiled algorithms, and show how tile-sizes may be selected at run-time to avoid self-interference. Subsequently Coleman and McKinley [6] generalized and improved the techniques of Lam *et al.*. Carter *et al.* [1] discuss hierarchical tiling schemes for a hierarchical shared memory model. Rivera and Tseng [18, 19] evaluate different heuristics for intra- and inter-array padding as a means of avoiding conflicts. Temam *et al.* have studied at data copying as a means to avoid cache interference in tiled loops [22]. Kodukula *et al.* have developed a seemingly flexible data-centric approach to loop tiling, called "shackling", which handles imperfect loop nests and may be used to tile for multiple levels of a memory hierarchy. The common focus on storage suggests that data shackling might be a suitable starting-point for developing more comprehensive optimization frameworks for the HAT-layout.

5. Conclusions

We have investigated a hierarchically tiled array layout, HAT, from a compiler perspective. The main advantage of this layout is that logical data locality in multi dimensional arrays consistently results in effective data locality at run-time, and that it makes compile-time analysis with respect to memory system performance feasible. This makes it possible to construct compilers which perform automatic tiling, and other compile-time optimizations, with a higher degree of accuracy and precision than allowed by linear array layouts.

With respect to cache hit rates, HAT inherently has a disadvantage for codes with regular array accesses. On the other hand, the HAT-layout makes codes with regular array accesses analyzable so that poor cache behavior can be detected and avoided at compile-time. A consequence of this is that the HAT-layout also could be interesting for applications where predictability is more important than average performance, such as in real-time systems.

Future work includes developing and evaluating automatic methods for selecting loop tile sizes and data copying, based on the information provided by the conflict vectors.

References

[1] Carter, L., Ferrante, J., and Hummel, S. (1995). Hierarchical tiling for improved superscalar performance. In *International Parallel Processing Symposium.*

[2] Chatterjee, S., Gilbert, J., Schreiber, R., and Teng, S.-H. (1992). Optimal evaluation of array expressions on massively parallel machines. Technical report, XEROX PARC.

[3] Chatterjee, S., Jain, V. V., Lebeck, A. R., Mundhra, S., and Thottethodi, M. (1999a). Nonlinear array layouts for hierarchical memory systems. In *Proc. 1999 ACM Int. Conf. on Supercomputing,* pages 444–453, Rhodes, Greece.

[4] Chatterjee, S., Lebeck, A. R., Patnala, P. K., and Thottethodi, M. (1999b). Recursive array layouts and fast parallel matrix multiplication. In *Proc. Eleventh ACM Symposium on Parallel Algorithms and Architectures,* pages 222–231, Saint-Malo, France.

[5] Cmelik, R. F. (1993). Spixtools user's manual. Technical Report SMLI TR-93-6, Sun Microsystems Labs, Mountain View, CA.

[6] Coleman, S. and McKinley, K. S. (1995). Tile size selection using cache organization and data layout. In *Proc. ACM Conf. on Programming Language Design and Implementation,* pages 279–290, La Jolla, CA.

[7] Drakenberg, N. P. (2001). *Hierarchical Array Tiling.* Licentiate thesis, Department of Teleinformatics, Royal

Institute of Technology, Stockholm. In preparation. http://www.it.kth.se/~npd/lic-thesis.ps.

[8] Gargantini, I. (1982). Linear octtrees for fast processing of three-dimensional objects. *Comput. Graphics Image Process.*, 20:365–374.

[9] Ghosh, S., Martonosi, M., and Malik, S. (1997). Cache miss equations: An analytical representation of cache misses. In *Proc. 1997 International Conference on Supercomputing*, pages 317–324, Vienna, Austria.

[10] Ghosh, S., Martonosi, M., and Malik, S. (1998). Precise miss analysis for program transformations with caches of arbitrary associativity. In *Proc. 8th Int. Conf. on Architectural Support for Programming Languages and Operating Systems*, Vienna, Austria.

[11] Gupta, M. (1992). *Automatic Data Partitioning on Distributed Memory Multicomputers.* PhD thesis, University of Illinios at Urbana-Champaign, Urbana, IL.

[12] Hu, Y., Johnsson, S., and Teng, S.-H. (1997). High Performance Fortran for highly irregular problems. In *Proc. Sixth ACM SIGPLAN Symp. on Principles and Practice of Parallel Programming*, pages 13–24, Las Vegas, NV.

[13] Knobe, K., Lucas, J. D., and Dally, W. J. (1992). Dynamic alignment on distributed memory systems. In *Proc. 3rd Workshop on Compilers for Parallel Computers*, pages 394–404.

[14] Lam, M. S., Rothberg, E. E., and Wolf, M. E. (1991). The cache performance and optimizations of blocked algorithms. In *Proc. 4th Int. Conf. on Architectural Support for Programming Languages and Operating Systems*, pages 63–74.

[15] Mitchell, N., Carter, L., and Ferrante, J. (1997). A compiler perspective on architectural evolutions. In *Workshop on Interaction between Compilers and Computer Architectures*, San Antonio, Texas.

[16] Morton, G. M. (1966). A computer oriented geodetic data base and a new technique in file sequencing. Technical report, IBM Ltd., Ottawa, Ontario.

[17] Pilkington, J. and Baden, S. (1996). Dynamic partitioning of non-uniform structured workloads with spacefilling curves. *IEEE Trans. on Parallel and Distributed Systems*, 7:288–300.

[18] Rivera, G. and Tseng, C.-W. (1998a). Data transformations for eliminating conflict misses. In *Proc. ACM SIGPLAN'98 Conference on Programming Language Design and Implementation*, pages 38–49, Montreal, Canada.

[19] Rivera, G. and Tseng, C.-W. (1998b). Eliminating conflict misses for high performance architectures. In *Proc. 1998 International Conference on Supercomputing*, pages 353–360, Melbourne, Australia.

[20] Schrack, G. (1992). Finding neighbors of equal size in linear quadtrees and octtrees in constant time. *CVGIP: Image Underst.*, 55(3):221–230.

[21] Schrijver, A. (1986). *Teory of Linear and Integer Programming.* John Wiley & Sons, Chichester.

[22] Temam, O., Granston, E. D., and Jalby, W. (1993). To copy or not to copy: A compile-time technique for assessing when data copying should be used to eliminate cache conflicts. In *Proc. Supercomputing '93*, Portland, OR.

[23] Tocher, K. (1954). The application of computers to sampling experiments. *J. Roy. Statist. Soc.*, 16(1):39–61.

[24] Vera, X., Llosa, J., Gonzalez, A., and Ciuraneta, C. (2000). A fast implementation of cache miss equations. In *Proc. 8th Workshop on Compilers for Parallel Computers*, pages 321–328, Aussois, France.

[25] Wise, D. S. (2000). Ahnentafel indexing into morton-ordered arrays, or matrix locality for free. In Bode, A. et al., editors, *Proc. Euro-Par 2000*, pages 774–783. Springer-Verlag.

[26] Wolfe, M. (1996). *High Performance Compilers for Parallel Computing.* Addison-Wesley, Redwood City, CA.

[27] Woodwark, J. R. (1982). The explicit quadtree as a structure for computer graphics. *Comput. J.*, 25(2):235–238.

Chapter 3

IMPACT OF TILE-SIZE SELECTION FOR SKEWED TILING

Yonghong Song
and Zhiyuan Li
Purdue University
{songyh,li}@cs.purdue.edu

Abstract

Tile-size selection is known to be a complex problem. This paper develops a new selection algorithm targeting relaxation codes. Unlike previous algorithms, this new algorithm considers the effect of loop skewing, which is necessary to tile such codes. It also estimates loop overhead and incorporates them into the execution cost model, which turns out to be critical to the decision between tiling a single loop level vs. tiling two loop levels. Our preliminary experimental results show a significant impact of these previously ignored issues on the execution time of tiled loops in relaxation codes. In our experiments, we measured the cache miss rate and the execution time of five benchmark programs on a single processor and we compared our algorithm with previous algorithms. Our algorithm achieves an average speedup of 1.27 to 1.63 over all the other algorithms.

Keywords: Data locality, loop skewing, loop tiling, optimizing compiler

1. Introduction

Memory access latency has become the key performance bottleneck on modern microprocessors. An important approach to reduce average latency is to exploit data locality on the cache memories and the translation lookaside buffer (TLB). *Tiling* is a well-known compiler technique to enhance data locality such that more data can be reused before they are replaced from the cache [24]. Tiling transforms a loop nest by combining strip-mining and loop interchange. *Loop skewing* and *loop reversal* are often used to enable tiling [21]. Figure 3.1 shows SOR relaxation as an example. Figure 3.1(a) shows the original loop nest in SOR, and Figure 3.1(b) shows the tiled SOR in which loop J is skewed with respect to loop T, and Figure 3.1(c) shows the tiled SOR in which loops J and I are skewed with respect to loop T.

Much of previous work on tiling applies to perfectly-nested loops only [8, 21, 22, 24]. Recently, we proposed a new technique to tile a class of imperfectly-nested loops [17, 18]. Performance of a tiled loop nest can vary dramatically with different tile sizes [9]. How to select proper tile sizes is hence an important issue. In this paper, if loop skewing is applied before tiling, such a tiling is called *skewed tiling*. All previous work tacitly assumes non-skewed tiling [4, 6, 9, 12, 16, 23]. However, such an assumption may not be true, especially for loops which perform iterative relaxation computations [17, 18]. Another important factor ignored in previous work is the loop overhead in terms of the increased instruction counts due to the increased loop levels. Further, tiling a software-pipelined loop will also increase the dynamic count of load instructions. In this paper, we shall show that these previously ignored factors can have a significant effect on tile-size selection.

In our recent work [17], we present a memory cost model to estimate cache misses, assuming that only one loop level is tiled. In this paper, we present a more general scheme by considering two loop levels which may both be tiled. We present an algorithm to compute tile sizes such that during each *tile traversal*, capacity misses and self-interference misses are eliminated. (Our tile-size selection algorithm is called STS.) Further, cross-interference misses are eliminated through array padding [15]. Given a tile size, we model the tiling cost based on both the number of cache misses and the loop overhead. To choose between tiling one loop level vs. tiling two loop levels, our algorithm computes their lowest costs and the respective tile sizes. We then choose the tiling level, and the corresponding best tile size, which yields the lowest cost. One can easily extend our discussion to higher loop levels, but such an extension does not seem useful for applications known to us.

In this paper, we consider data locality and performance enhancement on a single processor whose memory hierarchy includes cache memories at one or more levels. We have applied our tile-size selection algorithm to five numerical kernels, SOR, Jacobi, Livermore Loop No. 18 (LL18), `tomcatv` and `swim`, using a range of matrix sizes. We evaluate our algorithm on one processor of an SGI multiprocessor and on a SUN uniprocessor workstation. We compare our algorithm with TLI [3], TSS [4], LRW [9] and DAT [13]. Experiments show that our algorithm achieves an average speedup of 1.27 to 1.63 over all these previous algorithms.

```
DO T = 1, ITMAX
  DO J = 2, N - 1
    DO I = 2, N - 1
      A(I, J) =
          (A(I, J)
         + A(I + 1, J)
         + A(I - 1, J)
         + A(I, J + 1)
         + A(I, J - 1))/5
    END DO
  END DO
END DO
```

(a) Before transformation

```
DO JJ = 2, N - 1 + ITMAX, B1
  DO T = 1, ITMAX
    DO J = max(JJ - T, 2),
              min(JJ - T + B1 - 1, N - 1)
      DO I = 2, N - 1
        A(I, J) = A(I, J) + A(I + 1, J)
          +A(I - 1, J) + A(I, J + 1)
          +A(I, J - 1))/5
      END DO
    END DO
  EDN DO
END DO
```

(b) After skewing and "1-D" tiling

```
DO JJ = 2, N - 1 + ITMAX, B1
 DO II = 2, N - 1 + ITMAX, B2
  DO T = 1, ITMAX
   DO J = max(JJ - T, 2),
            min(JJ - T + B1 - 1, N - 1)
    DO I = max(II - T, 2),
             min(II - T + B2 - 1, N - 1)
      A(I, J) = A(I, J) + A(I + 1, J) + A(I - 1, J)
         +A(I, J + 1) + A(I, J - 1))/5
    END DO
   END DO
  EDN DO
 END DO
END DO
```

(c) After skewing and "2-D" tiling

Figure 3.1. An example of tiling: SOR relaxation.

In the rest of the paper, we first compare with related work in Section 2. We present a background in Section 3. We then present our memory cost model in Section 4. We model the execution time and present our tile-size selection algorithm in Section 5. In Section 6, we experimentally compare our algorithm with previous algorithms. Finally, we conclude in Section 7.

2. Related Work

2.1. Competing Tile-Size Selection Schemes

Several tile-size selection algorithms have been proposed previously: TLI by Chame and Moon [3], TSS by Coleman and McKinley [4] (and a variation of TSS by Rivera and Tseng [16]), LRW by Lam *et al.* [9] and DAT by Panda *et al.* [13]. These algorithms, although targeting more general programs than our STS algorithm, ignore loop skewing for relaxation codes when computing the tile size. They also only consider L1 data cache. However, STS considers L1 data cache , L2 cache and TLB.

Among all arrays in a tiled loop, LRW, TSS and TLI choose the tile size to eliminate certain kinds of cache misses due to a dominant ar-

Table 3.1. Comparison between various tile-size selection algorithms

	LRW	*TSS*	*TLI*	*STS*	*DAT*
Loop Skewing	No	No	No	Yes	No
L1 data cache	Yes	Yes	Yes	Yes	Yes
L2 cache & TLB	No	No	No	Yes	No
Dominant Array	Yes	Yes	Yes	No	No
Padding	No	No	No	Yes	Yes
Loop overhead	No	No	No	Yes	No
Tile shape	squ.	rect.	rect.	rect.	squ.
Tile dimensions	2	1,2	1,2	1,2	2

ray, while ignoring all other arrays. On the other hand, DAT and STS consider all arrays. Among all tile-size selection techniques, only DAT and STS utilizes padding, a data transformation technique to eliminate certain interference misses [15]. Only STS takes loop overhead into consideration, which is proven important by our experiments in Section 6. LRW and DAT requires a *square* tile shape, while TSS, TLI and STS allow a *rectangular* one. Consequently, the former only allow 2-D tiling, while the latter allow both 1-D and 2-D tiling. Table 4 summarizes the comparison between various algorithms, where "squ." means "square" and "rect." means "rectangular".

2.2. Other Related Work

Ghosh *et al.* estimate cache misses, given a tile size, for a perfect loop nest [6]. They also informally discuss a tile-size selection scheme using matrix multiplication as the example. No formal algorithm is presented, however. They do not discuss the estimation of cache misses for imperfectly-nested loops. Therefore, we are not able to compare with their method in our experiments.

Ferrante *et al.* present an algorithm to estimate the number of distinct cache lines over a perfect loop nest [5]. Temam *et al.* derive an analytical method to estimate the number of self-interference misses [20]. Mckinley *et al.* present a simple cost model to estimate the number of cache misses [11]. These methods do not consider the effect of loop skewing.

Rivera and Tseng present several padding algorithms to eliminate cache conflict misses [15, 16]. Manjikian and Abdelrahman use *cache partitioning* to scatter arrays evenly in the cache, such that cross-interference misses are minimized [10]. We use a different padding scheme which seems more suitable for our algorithm.

3. Background

In this section, we first define our program model and a few key parameters. We then discuss the issues of the memory hierarchy.

3.1. Skewed Tiling

Our program model allows a class of imperfectly-nested loops. Figure 3.2(a) shows a representative loop nest before tiling, where the T-loop body consists of m perfectly-nested loops. The depth of each perfectly-nested inner loop is at least two. The loop bounds L_{ij} and U_{ij}, $1 \leq i \leq m$, $j = 1, 2$, are T-invariant. We assume that the iteration space determined by J and I remains unchanged over different T-loop index values. For simplicity of presentation, we also assume that cache-line spatial locality is already fully exploited in the innermost loops except on the loop boundaries. Figure 3.2(b) shows the code after tiling the J_i loops only (*1-D tiling*), and Figure 3.2(c) shows the code after tiling both J_i and I_i loops (*2-D tiling*). In Figures 3.2(b) and 3.2(c), the iteration subspace defined by all J_i and I_i loops is called a *tile*. Loop T is called the *tile-sweeping* loop, and loops JJ and II are called the *tile-controlling* loops [21]. Each combination of JJ and II defines a *tile traversal*. Two tiles are said to be *consecutive* within a tile traversal if the difference of the corresponding T values equals 1. In this paper, we assume the data dependences permit both 1-D and 2-D tiling. Choosing between 1-D vs. 2-D tiling will depend on the estimate of cache misses and loop overhead. As far as estimating cache misses is concerned, 1-D tiling can be viewed as a special case of 2-D tiling with the maximum tile height. However, 2-D tiling incurs higher loop overhead, which we want to take into account.

Let $\gamma_1 = min\{L_{i1} | 1 \leq i \leq m\}$, $\gamma_2 = max\{U_{i1} | 1 \leq i \leq m\}$, $\eta_1 = min\{L_{i2} | 1 \leq i \leq m\}$ and $\eta_2 = max\{U_{i2} | 1 \leq i \leq m\}$. We call S_1 and S_2 the *skewing factors* corresponding to J_i and I_i loops respectively. (The skewing factors are also called the *slope* in our previous work [17, 18].) If $S_1 = 0$, then loop skewing is not applied before tiling at the J_i level. In this paper, we are interested only in skewed tiling at least at the J_i level, thus $S_1 > 0$. B_1 is called the *tile width* and B_2 is called the *tile height*. B_1 and B_2 are called the *tile size* collectively. These parameters are used to define the bounds of the tile-controlling loops. For reference, Tables 3.2 and 3.3 list all the symbols used in this paper and their brief descriptions.

For simplicity, we assume all arrays are of two dimensions with the same column sizes. (We assume column-major storage.) Lower dimension variables can be ignored due to their lesser impact on cache misses

```
DO T = 1, ITMAX
  DO J1 = L11, U11
    DO I1 = L12, U12
      ...
    END DO
  END DO
  ...
  DO Jm = Lm1, Um1
    DO Im = Lm2, Um2
      ...
    END DO
  END DO
END DO
```

(a)

```
DO JJ = γ1, γ2 + S1 * (ITMAX-1), B1
  DO T = f1(JJ), g1(JJ)
    DO J1 = L'11, U'11
      DO I1 = L12, U12
      END DO
    END DO
    ...
    DO Jm = L'm1, U'm1
      DO Im = Lm2, Um2
        ...
      END DO
    END DO
  END DO
END DO
```

(b)

```
DO JJ = γ1, γ2 + S1 * (ITMAX-1), B1
  DO II = η1, η2 + S2 * (ITMAX-1), B2
    DO T = f2(JJ, II), g2(JJ, II)
      DO J1 = L''11, U''11
        DO I1 = L''12, U''12
        END DO
      END DO
      ...
      DO Jm = L''m1, U''m1
        DO Im = L''m2, U''m2
          ...
        END DO
      END DO
    END DO
  END DO
END DO
```

(c)

Figure 3.2. The program model before and after tiling

in relaxation programs which we are interested in. Let n_a be the number of two dimensional arrays for the given tiled loop nest. Within the innermost loop I_i, $1 \le i \le m$, of the untiled program in Figure 3.2(a), we assume array subscript patterns of $A_k(I_i + a, J_i + b)$, $1 \le k \le n_a$, where a and b are known integer constants.

Although we restrict our program model to be either 1-D or 2-D tiling and restrict all arrays to be of two dimensions, such restrictions can be relaxed. We can have n-D tiling by extending our tiling technique in [18]. We can also allow high-dimensional arrays by extending our memory cost model and execution cost model. However, such extension to high-dimensional tiling and arrays seems unnecessary for the applications we currently have met.

Table 3.2. Description of symbols

Symbol	*Description*	*Symbol*	*Description*
S_1	The skewing factor for J_i loops	B_1	The tile width
S_2	The skewing factor for I_i loops	B_2	The tile height
N	The array column size	γ	$\gamma_2 - \gamma_1 + 1$
τ	Defined in Section 4	η	$\eta_2 - \eta_1 + 1$
n_1	Defined in Section 5.1	n_2	Defined in Section 5.1
n_3	Defined in Section 5.1	n_4	Defined in Section 5.1
n_5	Defined in Section 5.1	S_o	Defined in Section 4

3.2. Memory Hierarchy

The memory hierarchy includes registers, cache memories at one or more levels, the main memory and the secondary storage, as well as the TLB [7].

The TLB translates a virtual address into a physical address. The TLB has two key parameters, namely the *block count* T_c and the *block size* T_b. We call $T_s \equiv T_c T_b$ the TLB size. In this paper, T_b is the size of the virtual memory represented by each TLB entry in the number of data elements. We assume a fully-associative TLB with an LRU replacement policy.

For simplicity of presentation, we consider two levels of caches in this paper, namely the L1 and L2 caches, which are common in current practice. The L1 cache has several parameters, namely the *cache size* C_{s1}, the *cache block size* C_{b1} and the *set associativity* C_{a1}. C_{s1} and C_{b1} are measured in the number of data elements. Similarly for L2 cache, the cache size, cache block size and set associativity are C_{s2}, C_{b2} and C_{a2} respectively. The cache misses can be divided into three classes [7]: *compulsory misses*, *capacity misses* and *conflict misses.* Conflict misses can be attributed to self-interference misses of the same array and to cross-interference misses between different arrays.

4. A Memory Cost Model

In this section, we want to estimate the number of cache misses incurred by executing the loop nest in our program model after tiling.

Let S_o represent the iteration space defined by $\gamma_1 \leq J_i \leq \gamma_2$ and $\eta_1 \leq I_i \leq \eta_2$ in Figure 3.2(a). (For simplicity, we also regard S_o as the original iteration space defined by J_i and I_i loops in Figure 3.2(a), as if all J_i loops have the same loop bounds and all I_i loops have the same loop bounds.) S_o is illustrated in Figure 3.3(a) by the rectangle

Table 3.3. Description of symbols (cont.)

Symbol	*Description*
γ_1	The minimum lower bound of all J_i loops
γ_2	The maximum upper bound of all J_i loops
η_1	The minimum lower bound of all I_i loops
η_2	The maximum upper bound of all I_i loops
n_a	The number of arrays in the given loop nest
T_b	The number of data elements each TLB entry can represent
T_c	The number of TLB entries
T_s	The TLB size in the number of data elements
C_{s1}	The L1 cache size in the number of data elements
C_{b1}	The L1 cache line size in the number of data elements
C_{a1}	The L1 cache set associativity
C_{s2}	The L2 cache size in the number of data elements
C_{b2}	The L2 cache line size in the number of data elements
C_{a2}	The L2 cache set associativity
p_1	The L1 cache miss penalty
p_2	The L2 cache miss penalty
σ	The array footprint width constrained by the TLB (see Section 5.2.3)
ITMAX	The maximum index value for the tile-sweeping loop
W	The working-set size of the loop nest (Figure 3.2(a))

enclosed by the solid lines with the height η and the width γ. Within each tile traversal, we define the *base tile* to be a tile with $T = 1$ and an *advanced tile* to be a tile with $T > 1$. The dashed-lines in Figure 3.3(a) separate the base tiles of different tile traversals. The two shaded areas illustrate two different tile traversals, *tt1* and *tt2*, where each shaded rectangle with solid-line boundaries represents an advanced tile. When the tile-sweeping loop T increases the index by 1, the tiles can only overlap partially.

The cache misses incurred by one tile traversal can be partitioned into those within the base tile and those within the advanced tiles. Note that only those base tiles and advanced tiles overlapping with S_o will be executed, thus only they can contribute to the cache misses. In Figure 3.3(a), the base tile in the tile traversal *tt1* resides outside S_o, while the base tile in *tt2* resides within S_o.

We make the following two assumptions in our estimation of the number of cache misses:

- **Assumption 1:** There exist no cache reuse between different tile traversals.
- **Assumption 2:** $B_1 \ll \gamma$ and $B_1 \ll (ITMAX\text{-}1) * S_1$.

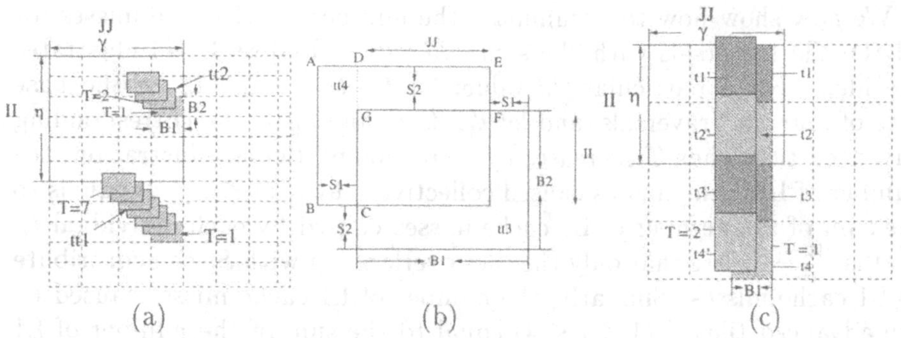

Figure 3.3. Illustration of tile traversal

Assumption 1 is reasonable if *ITMAX* is large, since it will be very likely for a tile traversal to overwrite cache lines whose old data could have been reused in the next tile traversal. Assumption 2 is reasonable because a large B_1 can easily cause an overflow in the TLB. As explained later in Section 4, our algorithm poses a constraint on B_1 such that TLB should not overflow. If the tile size (B_1, B_2) is chosen properly, there should be exactly one cache miss for each cache line accessed within a tile traversal. To be more specific, the following two properties should hold:

- **Property 1:** No capacity and self-interference misses are generated within a tile traversal.

- **Property 2:** No cross-interference misses are generated within a tile traversal.

In Section 5.2, we shall discuss how to preserve the above properties. For now, we assume they hold.

We first show how to compute the number of L1 cache misses caused by an advanced tile. Let W represent the size of the data set accessed by the original loop nest in terms of the number of data elements. The average size of the data accessed by one tile is estimated to be $D = \frac{W}{\gamma\eta} * B_1 B_2$. Figure 3.3(b) shows two consecutive tiles, *tt3* and *tt4*, within a tile traversal, assuming that both tiles reside within S_o. The iteration subspace of *tt4* is produced by shifting the iteration subspace of *tt3* upwards by S_2 iterations and to the left by S_1 iterations. The L1 cache misses in *tt4* either occur in Region ABCD or in Region DEFG. The total estimated L1 cache misses equal to $(S_1 B_2 + S_2 B_1 - S_1 S_2) * \frac{W}{\gamma\eta C_{b1}}$. (This estimate may not be exact because data accessed at the lower border of Region DEFG may or may not be in the cache already.)

We now show how to accumulate the number of L1 cache misses for all the tile traversals with the same JJ value. Figure 3.3(c) illustrates the idea. For a particular JJ value, let t_1, t_2, t_3 and t_4 be the base tiles of four tile traversals, and let t'_1, t'_2, t'_3 and t'_4 be the corresponding advanced tiles when T increases by 1. In this particular illustration, the number of L1 cache misses caused collectively by t_i $(1 \leq i \leq 4)$ equals to the sum of the number of L1 cache misses caused by each individual t_i, that is, $\frac{WB_1}{\gamma C_{b1}}$. Note that only the tiles overlapping with S_o can contribute to L1 cache misses. Similarly, the number of L1 cache misses caused by the advanced tiles t'_i $(1 \leq i \leq 4)$ equal to the sum of the number of L1 cache misses caused by individual t'_i, that is, $\frac{S_1W}{\gamma C_{b1}} + 2(B_1 - S_1)S_2 * \frac{W}{\gamma\eta C_{b1}}$. In general, the number of L1 cache misses caused by the advanced tiles with the same JJ value equal to $\frac{S_1W}{\gamma C_{b1}} + \tau(B_1 - S_1)S_2 * \frac{W}{\gamma\eta C_{b1}}$, where τ is the number of base tiles in S_o for a particular JJ estimated as

$$\tau = \begin{cases} \lceil \frac{\eta}{B_2} \rceil & \text{if } 1 \leq B_2 < \eta + S_2 * (\text{ITMAX-1}) \\ 0 & \text{if } B_2 = \eta + S_2 * (\text{ITMAX-1}) \end{cases}$$

The value $\eta + S_2 * (ITMAX\text{-}1)$ is the maximum height of the iteration space after tiling. Any B_2 value greater than or equal to $\eta + S_2 *$ $(ITMAX\text{-}1)$ results in no tiling at the I_i loop level.

With Assumptions 1 and 2 and Properties 1 and 2 standing, we have the following formulas to estimate the number of cache misses. Their derivation can found in [19].

The total number of L1 cache misses for 2-D tiling is approximately

$$\frac{WS_1(ITMAX\text{-}1)}{C_{b1}B_1} + \frac{WS_2(ITMAX\text{-}1)}{C_{b1}B_2}. \tag{3.1}$$

The number of L2 cache misses for 2-D tiling is approximately

$$\frac{WS_1(ITMAX\text{-}1)}{C_{b2}B_1} + \frac{WS_2(ITMAX\text{-}1)}{C_{b2}B_2}. \tag{3.2}$$

With 1-D tiling (in Figure 3.2(c)), the L1 cache temporal locality is not exploited across the T-loop iterations. The number of L1 cache misses is approximately

$$ITMAX * \frac{W}{C_{b1}}. \tag{3.3}$$

The total number of cache misses for the L2 cache is approximately

$$\frac{WS_1(ITMAX\text{-}1)}{C_{b2}B_1}. \tag{3.4}$$

5. Tile-Size Selection

In this section, we first present an execution cost model for tiling with a given tile size, based on both the number of cache misses and the loop overhead. We then present our tile-size selection algorithm, followed by a running example to go through our algorithm.

5.1. An Execution Cost Model for Tiling

Loop tiling introduces loop overhead. To decide between 1-D tiling and 2-D tiling, the overhead of the tiled I_i loops in Figure 3.2(c) needs to be measured. Let n_1 be the sum of the static number of instructions for the computation of all the I_i loop bounds $(1 \leq i \leq m)$. The I_i loop overhead due to 2-D tiling in terms of the dynamic count of instructions, is measured approximately by

$$n_1 * \frac{ITMAX * \gamma * \eta}{B_2}. \tag{3.5}$$

Let n_2 be the sum of the static number of instructions in the I_i $(1 \leq i \leq m)$ loop bodies. The dynamic instruction count for the I_i loop bodies is

$$n_2 * ITMAX * \gamma * \eta. \tag{3.6}$$

From (3.5) and (3.6), if n_1 and n_2 are approximately equal, then a small B_2 will introduce large loop overhead. Let n_3 be sum of the static number of instructions for the computation of all the J_i loop bounds $(1 \leq i \leq m)$. The loop overhead due to tiled J_i loops can be measured by

$$n_3 * \frac{ITMAX * \gamma}{B_1}. \tag{3.7}$$

Enabled by scalar replacement [2], in a software-pipelined loop [1], loaded data can be reused in different iterations. The dynamic count of load instructions can hence be reduced. Let n_4 be the sum of the static count of load instructions in the prologues and the epilogues of all the software-pipelined loops. Let n_5 be the sum of the number of load instructions divided by the unroll factor in the software-pipelined loop bodies. The unroll factor is one if the loop is not unrolled. The dynamic count of load instruction with 1-D tiling is approximately

$$(n_4 + n_5\gamma)\eta * ITMAX. \tag{3.8}$$

With 2-D tiling, the dynamic count of load instructions is approximately

$$(n_4 + n_5 B_2) * \frac{\gamma}{B_2} * \eta * ITMAX = (n_4 \frac{\gamma}{B_2} + n_5\gamma)\eta * ITMAX. \quad (3.9)$$

Clearly, if n_4 is significantly greater than n_5 and B_2 is small, then the dynamic count of load instructions with 2-D tiling can be much greater than that with 1-D tiling.

Let p_1 be the penalty for an L1 cache miss and p_2 be the penalty for an L2 cache miss. By adding the penalty due to L1 cache misses in Formula (3.3), the penalty due to L2 cache misses in Formula (3.4), the loop overhead due to tiled J_i loops in Formula (3.7), and the dynamic count of load instructions for software-pipelined innermost loops in Formula (3.8), we can model the execution cost for 1-D tiling by

$$p_1 * (ITMAX * \frac{W}{C_{b1}}) + p_2 * (\frac{WS_1(ITMAX\text{-}1)}{C_{b2}B_1})$$

$$+n_3\frac{ITMAX * \gamma}{B_1} + (n_4 + n_5\gamma)\eta * ITMAX. \quad (3.10)$$

In the above formula, we assume the latency of one unit of time for each instruction, including a load instruction. From (3.10), with 1-D tiling, we want to maximize B_1 (subject to Properties 1 and 2 aforementioned) such that the number of L2 cache misses is minimized. By adding the penalty due to L1 cache misses in Formula (3.1), the penalty due to L2 cache misses in Formula (3.2), the dynamic count of load instructions for software-pipelined innermost loops in Formula (3.9), the loop overhead due to tiled J_i loops in Formula (3.7), and the loop overhead due to the tiled innermost loop in Formula (3.5), the execution cost for 2-D tiling can be modeled by

$$p_1 * (\frac{WS_1(ITMAX\text{-}1)}{C_{b1}B_1} + \frac{WS_2(ITMAX\text{-}1)}{C_{b1}B_2}) + p_2 * (\frac{WS_1(ITMAX\text{-}1)}{C_{b2}B_1} + \frac{WS_2(ITMAX\text{-}1)}{C_{b2}B_2}) + n_1 * \frac{ITMAX * \gamma * \eta}{B_2} + n_3\frac{ITMAX * \gamma}{B_1}$$

$$+(n_4\frac{\gamma}{B_2} + n_5\gamma)\eta * ITMAX. \quad (3.11)$$

5.2. Tile-Size Selection Algorithm

In this section, we first discuss how to preserve Properties 1 and 2. We then present our tile-size selection algorithm.

```
Procedure EnumFPSize(Cs, Cb, N)
  for F2 ← 1 to N do
    F1 ← 1
    t ← (F1 * N) mod Cs
    while ((F2 + Cb − 1) ≤ t ≤ (Cs − F2 − Cb + 1))
      Record (F1, F2)
      F1 ← F1 + 1
      t ← (F1 * N) mod Cs
    end while
  end for
```

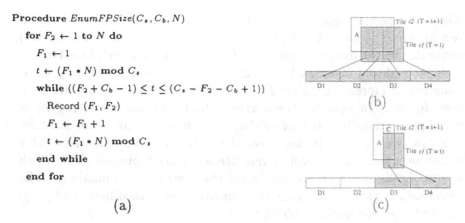

(a)

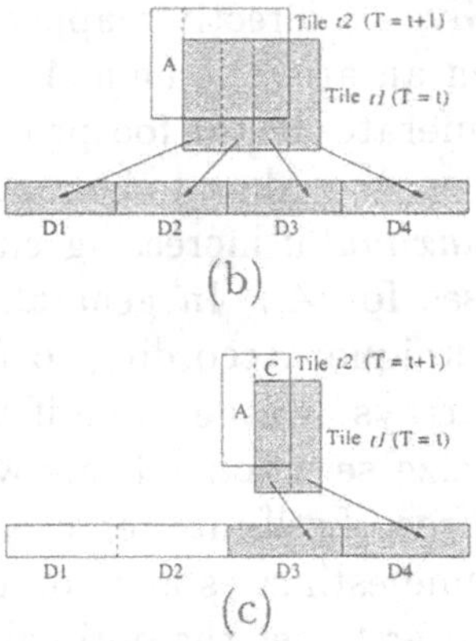

Figure 3.4. Procedure *EnumFPSize* and an illustration of utilizing portions of the cache by a single tile

5.2.1 Preserving Property 1. First, we discuss how to eliminate self-interference misses within a single tile. For any array A_i, let R be the minimum rectangular array region which contains all the A_i elements referenced within a tile t. We say that A_i's footprint size within tile t is (F_1, F_2), where F_1 and F_2 are the numbers of columns and rows in R respectively. We call F_1 (F_2) the *array footprint width (height)* for A_i within tile t. Reversely, given a footprint size of A_i, the tile size can also be computed. Given the subscript patterns and the loop bounds, such a computation is straightforward and we omit the details. For the example of SOR (Figure 3.1(c)), assuming the array footprint size for A to be (κ_1, κ_2), the loop tile size should be $(\kappa_1 - 2, \kappa_2 - 2)$. For array A_i, if the footprint height F_2 is greater than the distance between the locations of two columns in the cache, then the columns accessed within the tile will conflict in the cache, creating self-interference misses [3]. More precisely, we have the following lemma:

Lemma 1 Given array footprint size (F_1, F_2) for any A_i $(1 \le i \le n_a)$, a cache of size C_s and cache line size C_b, if there exist no self-interference misses, then the distance between the starting cache locations of any two columns of A_i within F_1 consecutive columns is either no smaller than F_2, or no greater than $C_s - F_2$. Conversely, there exist no self-interference misses if the distance between the starting cache locations of any two columns of A_i within F_1 consecutive columns is either no smaller than $F_2 + C_b - 1$, or no greater than $C_s - F_2 - C_b + 1$.
Proof Obvious. ◇

Given a directly-mapped cache of size C_s and cache line size C_b, and given an array column size N, procedure *EnumFPSize* in Figure 3.4(a) enumerates all the footprint sizes (F_1, F_2) which incur no self-interference misses, according to Lemma 1. We say that a footprint size (F_1, F_2) of A_i is *maximal* if increasing either F_1 or F_2 will introduce self-interference misses for A_i. In general, the maximal footprint size for array A_i is not unique. According to *EnumFPSize*, the maximal footprint sizes for all arrays are the same if they have the same array column sizes. Our tile-size selection scheme will enumerate all array footprint sizes which are free of self-interference misses until the sizes become maximal. The scheme estimates and compares the execution cost for different (F_1, F_2) in order to get the optimal tile size.

Next, suppose the cache is not directly-mapped, and assume an LRU replacement policy. We show that the parameter C_s in procedure *EnumFPSize* should not be the whole cache size. Otherwise, self-interference misses will occur when the execution proceeds from one tile to the next. For clarity, instead of arguing formally for the general cases, we illustrate the cases of 2-way and fully-associative caches. Figure 3.4(b) shows two consecutive tiles *t1* and *t2*. Suppose C_s equals the whole cache size in procedure *EnumFPSize* and suppose the footprint size of *t1* is maximal. Tile *t1* accesses the cache from the least-recently referenced data segment to the most-recently referenced data segment in the memory, in the order of *D1*, *D2*, *D3* and *D4* which are separated by solid lines. If the cache associativity is $C_{a1} = 2$, then *D2* and *D4* will map to the same cache sets. The data accessed in the blank rectangle A will replace segment *D2*. If the cache is fully associative, *D1* will be replaced. However, part of the old data in segment *D2* (or *D1*) could have been reused by tile *t2*. One solution to avoid the replacement of useful data is to reduce the footprint size within *t1* such that only a portion of the cache is used to compute the maximal footprint size in *EnumFPSize*. Figure 3.4(c) shows the case for two-way set-associative cache. In this way, the data accessed in Regions A and C will replace the cache segment *D2* and part of segment *D1*, whose old data are not reused by *t2*. The reusable data in *D3* will be kept in the cache. Using the above idea, we let $C_s = \frac{C_{a1}-1}{C_{a1}} C_{s1}$ in procedure *EnumFPSize*, for 2-way and fully-associative caches. The cases of other associativities are more complex, and they will not be discussed in this paper.

To eliminate capacity misses, the footprint size of each array A_i can only be $(\lfloor \frac{F_1}{n_a} \rfloor, F_2)$, a fraction of (F_1, F_2). Here, we choose to partition columns instead of rows, in order to preserve spatial locality. Assume that $(B_1^{(i)}, B_2^{(i)})$, $1 \leq i \leq n_a$, is the tile size such that the footprint size for array A_i within a single tile is $(\lfloor \frac{F_1}{n_a} \rfloor, F_2)$. For 2-way and fully-

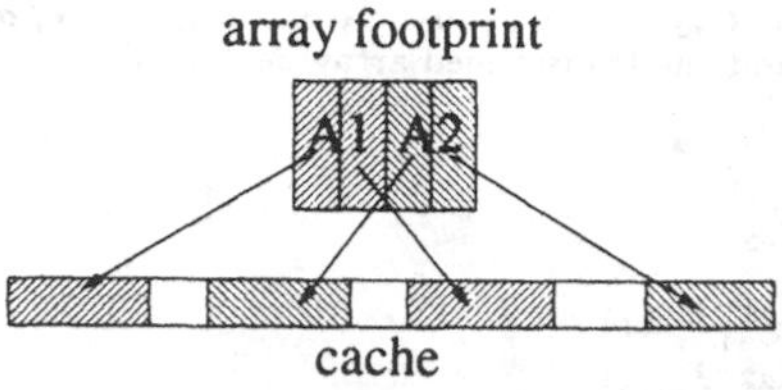

Figure 3.5. An illustration of padding to eliminate cross-interferences

associative caches, we choose the tile size for the tiled loop as $(B_1, B_2) = (min_i B_1^{(i)}, min_i B_2^{(i)})$. For directly-mapped caches, we choose $(B_1, B_2) = (min_i B_1^{(i)} - S_1, min_i B_2^{(i)} - S_2)$. One can prove that for directly-mapped, 2-way and fully-associative caches, Property 1 holds under the above treatment. For other set-associative caches, procedure *EnumFPSize* needs to be revised.

5.2.2 Preserving Property 2. We apply inter-array padding to eliminate cross-interference misses within a tile traversal. For simplicity of presentation, we assume that the array subscript patterns of one particular array A_k cover all the array subscript patterns for all the other arrays A_i, $i \neq k$. The discussion in this section can be easily extended if such an assumption does not hold. Using inter-array padding, we let the starting addresses for array $A_i (1 \leq i \leq n_a)$ map to the same location in the cache as the starting address of the $(\lfloor \frac{W}{n_a} \rfloor * (i-1))$th column of array A_1. With such padding, cross-interference misses are eliminated within a single tile between A_i and A_j $(1 \leq i, j \leq n_a, i \neq j)$.

When the execution goes from one tile to the next, if the cache is directly-mapped, the newly accessed data for A_i will map to cache locations previously unused in the tile traversal. If the cache is not directly-mapped, the newly accessed data for A_i will map to cache locations which are either previously unused or will not be referenced again within the current traversal. Therefore, cross-interference misses are also eliminated within a tile traversal. Figure 3.5 illustrates an example for $F_1 = 4$ and $n_a = 2$, where the cache is directly mapped. Here, assuming the starting address for array A_1 to be 0, the padded number of data items, x, between arrays A_1 and A_2 can be determined from

$$(size(A_1) + x) = (2 * N), \ \mathbf{mod} \ C_{s1}. \tag{3.12}$$

We are ready to present our tile-size selection algorithm in the next section.

Input: S_1, S_2, C_{s1}, C_{a1}, C_{b1}, C_{s2}, C_{a2}, C_{b2}, n_1, n_3, n_4, n_5, n_a, N, σ (see Tables 3.2 and 3.3).
Output: Tile size (B_1, B_2) and the transformed array declaration.
Procedure:

```
if (C_a1 = 1) then
    ComputeTileSize-2D(C_s1)
    ComputeTileSize-1D(C_s2)
else
    ComputeTileSize-2D(((C_a1 - 1)/C_a1) C_s1)
    ComputeTileSize-1D(((C_a2 - 1)/C_a2) C_s2)
end if
Apply inter-array padding (see Section 5.2.2).
Return (B_1, B_2).

Procedure ComputeTileSize-1D(C_s)
  /* (TB_1, TB_2) is a temporary tile size. */
  Select the maximum tile width κ such that the footprint of
     one tile can fit in both the TLB and the L2 cache.
  TB_1 ← κ - S_1, TB_2 ← η + S_2 * (ITMAX-1)
  Compute the execution cost, TM, based on (3.10).
  if (TM < M) then B_1 ← TB_1, B_2 ← TB_2, M ← TM end if

Procedure ComputeTileSize-2D(C_s)
  /* (TB_1, TB_2) is a temporary tile size. */
  M ← ∞
  for F_2 ← C_b1 to N do
    F_1 ← 1
    t ← (F_1 * N) mod C_s
    while (F_1 ≤ σ or (F_2 + C_b1 - 1) ≤ t ≤ (C_s - F_2 - C_b1 + 1))
    do
      Convert array footprint size (F_1, F_2) to loop tile size
         (TB_1, TB_2) (see Section 5.2.1).
      if (C_a1 = 1) then
        TB_1 ← TB_1 - S_1, TB_2 ← TB_2 - S_2
      end if
      if (TB_1 > 0 and TB_2 > 0) then
        Compute the execution cost, TM, based on (3.11).
        if (TM < M) then
          B_1 ← TB_1, B_2 ← TB_2, M ← TM
        end if
      end if
      F_1 ← F_1 + 1
      t ← (F_1 * N) mod C_s
    end while
  end for
```

Figure 3.6. Tile-size selection algorithm - STS

5.2.3 Algorithm STS. Algorithm *STS* in Figure 3.6 selects the tile size by interleaving the operations in procedure *EnumFPSize* with the applications of Formulas (3.10) and (3.11) which compute the execution cost. We require B_2 to be no smaller than the cache line size C_{b1}. However, we do not require B_2 to be a multiple of C_{b1}, since such a requirement does not have much benefit when execution proceeds from one tile to the next. In addition to the conditions stated in procedure *EnumFPSize*, the array footprint width F_2 should be no greater than σ, which is the total number of array columns representable by the TLB minus the number of newly accessed array columns when the execution proceeds from one tile to the next.

Table 3.4. Machine parameters

	C_{s1}	C_{b1}	C_{a1}	C_{s2}	C_{b2}	C_{a2}	T_c	T_b	p_1	p_2
Ultra II	2K	2	1	256K	8	1	64	1K	6	45
R10K	4K	4	2	512K	16	2	64	4K	9	68

STS makes the decision between 1-D and 2-D tiling based on their execution cost. For 1-D tiling, *ComputeTileSize-1D* tries to find tile width B_1 such that Properties 1 and 2 are preserved on the L2 cache and that Formula (3.10) is minimized. For 2-D tiling, *ComputeTileSize-2D* enumerates all tile sizes which are free of self-interference misses. The tile size with the lowest execution cost is selected. Between 1-D and 2-D tiling, the scheme with the lower execution cost is chosen.

STS needs a conversion from array footprint size (F_1, F_2) to loop tile size (B_1, B_2), as stated in Section 5.2.1. If the resulting tile width or tile height is nonpositive, 1-D tiling is chosen.

The complexity of STS is $O(N * min(C_{s1}, \sigma)) = O(N\sigma)$. (In practice, σ is much smaller than the L1 cache size C_{s1}.)

5.3. A Running Example

We now take SOR (Figure 3.1) as an example to show how STS works, assuming the following parameters: $N = 1000$, $ITMAX = 1050$, $C_{s1} = 4096$, $C_{b1} = 4$, $C_{a1} = 2$, $C_{s2} = 128 * 1024$, $C_{b2} = 16$, $C_{a2} = 2$, $T_b = 4096$ and $T_c = 48$, $n_1 = 15$, $n_3 = 15$, $n_4 = 20$, $n_5 = 3$, $p_1 = 6$, and $p_2 = 30$. Based on the array subscripts and the loop bounds, we have $S_1 = S_2 = 1$, $\gamma = \eta = 999$, $W = N * N = 1000000$ and $\sigma = 195$.

In the following, we show the steps of STS.

- Since $C_a = 2$, *ComputeTileSize-2D*$(\frac{C_{s1}}{2})$ is called, and we have $B_1 = 38$, $B_2 = 43$. The execution cost for 2-D tiling is $M = 4171464893$ units based on Formula (3.11).

- *ComputeTileSize-1D*$(\frac{C_{s2}}{2})$ computes $TB_1 = 63$, $TB_2 = 2048$. The execution cost for 1-D tiling is $TM = 4764840588$ units based on Formula (3.10). In this case, STS favors 2-D tiling over 1-D tiling with the tile size $(38, 43)$.

- No inter-array padding is applied since $n_a = 1$.

6. Experimental Evaluation

We apply our tile-size selection algorithm STS to three numerical kernels, SOR, Jacobi and Livermore Loop No. 18 (LL18), and two SPEC benchmarks, `tomcatv` and `swim`. These benchmarks are chosen because they require skewed tiling. We use reference inputs for `tomcatv` and `swim`. For SOR, Jacobi and LL18, we declare $N \times N$ double precision arrays, with randomly chosen N based on a random number generator [14] with the following formula

$$z_{n+1} = (16807 z_n) \bmod 2147483647. \tag{3.13}$$

Assuming that the array sizes under consideration range from r_0 to r_1, we select 200 array sizes, a_n, such that

$$a_n = r_0 + (z_n \bmod (r_1 - r_0)), 1 \leq n \leq 200. \tag{3.14}$$

We use $z_1 = 9$ in all our experiments. Note that it would be too time-consuming to exhaustly test all array sizes within the range in our experiments.

We run the test programs on a SUN Ultra II uniprocessor workstation and on one MIPS R10K processor of an SGI Origin 2000 multiprocessor, with the tile sizes selected by five different algorithms, namely, STS, TLI [3], TSS [4], LRW [9] and DAT [13]. In this paper, we only show the summarized results. The raw experimental results can be found in [19]. In order to handle several equally-important arrays, we make an obviously necessary modification on the original TSS and LRW algorithms such that the value of the initial tile size will meet the working set constraint. We also modify the TLI algorithm such that only the cache size divided by the number of equally-important arrays is used to compute the tile sizes which are free of self-interference misses. If any algorithm decides to choose the whole array column as the tile height, then we let $B_2 = \eta + S_2 * (\text{ITMAX-1})$ and tile the J_i loops only (Figure 3.2(b)).

Table 3.4 lists the machine parameters for the Ultra II and the R10K, assuming the size of an array element of 8 bytes. The main memory size for the Ultra II is 128M bytes, and it is 16G bytes for the R10K. To accommodate the competition between instructions and data in the L2 cache, we only tries to utilize 95% of the total L2 cache capacity. We use the machine counters on the R10K to measure the cache miss rate. Currently, we obtain the values of n_1, n_3, n_4 and n_5 by examining the assembly code of the original program. A backend compiler can easily obtain such numbers.

On the R10K, the untiled codes are compiled using the native compiler with the "-O3" optimization switch set. On the R10K, we found that

Table 3.5. Speedup by STS and average cache miss rates for different schemes for SOR

Ultra II	*ORG*	*LRW*	*TSS*	*TLI*	*STS*	*DAT*
Speedup by STS	1.10	1.06	1.34	1.03	1.00	1.10
L1 Miss Rate	0.14	0.02	0.07	0.03	0.02	0.06
L2 Miss Rate	0.066	0.006	0.009	0.005	0.006	0.008
R10K	*ORG*	*LRW*	*TSS*	*TLI*	*STS*	*DAT*
Speedup by STS	1.26	0.99	1.06	0.98	1.00	0.97
L1 Miss Rate	0.113	0.006	0.024	0.012	0.008	0.031
L2 Miss Rate	0.116	0.057	0.030	0.031	0.085	0.007

compiling the tiled code with the "-O2" switch can sometimes run faster than that with the "-O3" switch, regardless of the tile-size selection schemes. Therefore, we compile the tiled code with "-O2" or "-O3" depending on which produces shorter execution time. For all the tile-size selection schemes, we switch off loop tiling for the native compiler on the R10K when we compile the tiled source programs (with for both 1-D and 2-D tiling). We switch off prefetching on the R10K when we compile 2-D tiled source codes since prefetching may increase cross-interference misses for smaller tile height B_2. We also switch off common block reorganization since the tile size selection algorithms already take care of memory layout. On the Ultra II, both the untiled and the tiled codes are compiled using the native compiler with the "-fast -xchip=ultra2 -xarch=v8plusa -fsimple=2" optimization switch, which is recommended by the vendor.

The SOR kernel We fix *ITMAX* to 1050 and randomly choose 200 array sizes ranging from 200 to 2000, i.e., $(r_0, r_1) = (200, 2000)$ in Equation (3.14). The skewing factors are $S_1 = S_2 = 1$. We have $n_1 = n_3 = 11$, $n_4 = 9$ and $n_5 = 3$. Table 3.5 summarizes the average speedup by STS over other schemes, average L1 and L2 cache miss rates for SOR. The execution time is averaged by geometric mean, and the cache miss rates are averaged by arithmetic mean of cache miss rates for individual array size.

The Jacobi Kernel We fix *ITMAX* to 500 and randomly choose 200 array sizes ranging from 200 to 2000. The skewing factors are $S_1 = S_2 = 1$. We have $n_1 = n_3 = 17$, $n_4 = 28$ and $n_5 = 10$. Table 3.6 shows the average speedup by STS, average L1 and L2 cache miss rates for Jacobi.

Table 3.6. Speedup by STS and average cache miss rates for different schemes for Jacobi

Ultra II	*ORG*	*LRW*	*TSS*	*TLI*	*STS*	*DAT*
Speedup by STS	5.40	1.39	2.17	1.28	1.00	1.10
L1 Miss Rate	0.60	0.12	0.24	0.24	0.06	0.19
L2 Miss Rate	0.15	0.02	0.02	0.01	0.02	0.01
R10K	*ORG*	*LRW*	*TSS*	*TLI*	*STS*	*DAT*
Speedup by STS	5.46	0.98	1.21	1.15	1.00	0.97
L1 Miss Rate	0.234	0.022	0.062	0.144	0.038	0.082
L2 Miss Rate	0.169	0.066	0.043	0.006	0.104	0.010

Table 3.7. Speedup by STS and average cache miss rates for different schemes for LL18

Ultra II	*ORG*	*LRW*	*TSS*	*TLI*	*STS*	*DAT*
Speedup by STS	1.89	2.92	2.54	1.96	1.00	2.11
L1 Miss Rate	0.435	0.217	0.284	0.326	0.469	0.208
L2 Miss Rate	0.112	0.037	0.056	0.019	0.018	0.021
R10K	*ORG*	*LRW*	*TSS*	*TLI*	*STS*	*DAT*
Speedup by STS	1.72	1.98	1.98	1.62	1.00	1.69
L1 Miss Rate	0.173	0.072	0.096	0.122	0.217	0.066
L2 Miss Rate	0.128	0.049	0.075	0.010	0.005	0.026

The `LL18` Kernel LL18 has 9 arrays, and the tiled version has 11 arrays after duplicating *ZR* and *ZZ*. Due to the relatively large number of arrays, the array sizes we used in SOR will produce extremely small tile sizes for all the tile-size selection schemes. Therefore, we reduce the array sizes and randomly choose 200 array sizes ranging from 200 to 500. We fix *ITMAX* to 300. The skewing factors are $S_1 = S_2 = 2$. We have $n_1 = n_3 = 75$, $n_4 = 100$ and $n_5 = 35$. Table 3.7 shows the average speedup by STS, average L1 and L2 cache miss rates for LL18.

`tomcatv` The program `tomcatv` can only be tiled with one dimension [18], hence only STS can be applied for tile-size selection. We use two different reference inputs from SPEC92 and SPEC95 respectively. To verify whether STS produces nearly the best results, we run through a range of tile sizes, from 2 to three times of the size selected by STS, for each version of `tomcatv`. The results chosen by STS are closer to the optimal solutions than to the original programs [19]. To examine how padding will affect the STS, we also run both versions of `tomcatv` without padding applied. Except few cases, padded version runs significantly

Table 3.8. Summary of speedup of STS over other schemes

	ORG	*LRW*	*TSS*	*TLI*	*DAT*
Ultra II	2.24	1.63	1.95	1.37	1.37
R10K	2.28	1.24	1.36	1.22	1.17
Both	2.26	1.42	1.63	1.29	1.27

faster than unpadded version [19], which demonstrates the effectiveness of padding for STS.

`swim` Similar to `tomcatv`, `swim` is tiled only with one dimension. On the R10K, we use three different reference inputs from SPEC92, SPEC95 and SPEC2000 respectively. On the Ultra II, however, because of the large data set size and the relative small main memory size, the SPEC2000 version of `swim` cannot be tiled with a positive tile size, i.e., it cannot be tiled profitably. Hence, on the Ultra II, we use two different reference inputs from SPEC92 and SPEC95 respectively. Similar to `tomcatv`, we choose the tile sizes from 2 to three times of the size selected by STS for each version of `swim`. The results chosen by STS are closer to the optimal solutions than to the original programs [19]. Similar to `tomcatv`, padded version runs faster than unpadded version in most cases [19].

6.1. Discussion

In summary, Table 3.8 shows the speedup by STS over all the other schemes for all 600 cases for SOR, Jacobi and LL18, where "Both" stands for both the Ultra II and the R10K.

One interesting point is related with LRW. Considering the combination of each benchmark (SOR, Jacobi and LL18) and each machine (Ultra II and R10K), LRW produces equal or smaller average L1 cache misses in 5 out of 6 combinations compared with STS. However, this does not translate into large performance saving. (The worst average speed ratio of STS over LRW is 0.98.) We found that in general LRW produces smaller tile sizes than STS, which potentially introduces more loop overhead. For LL18, LRW has greater average L2 cache miss rates than STS since STS exploits locality for L2 cache in most of cases due to large number of arrays.

7. Conclusion

In this paper, we present a memory cost model to predict the cache misses after skewed tiling. Further, we model the execution cost by considering both the cache misses and the loop overhead, based on which we make a decision between tiling one loop level vs. two loop levels. We present Algorithm STS, which selects the tile size such that the capacity misses and self-interference misses within a tile traversal are eliminated. STS uses inter-array padding to eliminate cross-interference misses. We also compare STS with four previous algorithms, TLI, TSS, LRW and DAT. Experiments show that STS achieves an average speedup of 1.27 to 1.63 over all the other four algorithms. We have previously implemented a cost model along with a number of tiling algorithms within a research compiler [18]. However, we are yet to implement the cost model presented in this paper. Ideally, our cost model should be incorporated in a backend compiler, which will be our future work.

In our experiments, we found that turning on the compiler switch for prefetching for the tiled codes may degrade the performance. How to effectively combine tiling and prefetching seems an interesting future research topic.

Acknowledgments

This work is sponsored in part by National Science Foundation through grants ACI-0082834, CCR-9975309 and MIP-9610379, by Indiana 21st Century Fund, by Purdue Research Foundation, and by a donation from Sun Microsystems, Inc.

References

[1] Allan, V., Jones, R., Lee, R., and Allan, S. (1993). Software pipelining. *ACM Computing Surveys*, 27(3):367–432.

[2] Callahan, D., Carr, S., and Kennedy, K. (1990). Improving register allocation for subscripted variables. In *Proceedings of ACM SIGPLAN 1990 Conference on Programming Language Design and Implementation*, pages 53–65, White Plains, New York.

[3] Chame, J. and Moon, S. (1999). A tile selection algorithm for data locality and cache interference. In *Proceedings of the Thirteenth ACM International Conference on Supercomputing*, pages 492–499, Rhodes, Greece.

[4] Coleman, S. and McKinley, K. S. (1995). Tile size selection using cache organization and data layout. In *Proceedings of ACM SIGPLAN*

Conference on Programming Language Design and Implementation, pages 279–290, La Jolla, CA.

[5] Ferrante, J., Sarkar, V., and Thrash, W. (1991). On estimating and enhancing cache effectiveness. In *Proceedings of the Fourth International Workshop on Languages and Compilers for Parallel Computing.* Also in *Lecture Notes in Computer Science*, pp. 328-341, Springer-Verlag, August 1991.

[6] Ghosh, S., Martonosi, M., and Malik, S. (1998). Precise miss analysis for program transformations with caches of arbitrary associativity. In *Proceedings of the Eighth ACM Conference on Architectural Support for Programming Languages and Operating Systems*, pages 228–239, San Jose, California.

[7] Hennessy, J. and Patterson, D. (1996). *Computer Architecture: A Quantitative Approach.* Morgan Kaufmann Publishers.

[8] Kodukula, I., Ahmed, N., and Pingali, K. (1997). Data-centric multi-level blocking. In *Proceedings of ACM SIGPLAN Conference on Programming Language Design and Implementation*, pages 346–357, Las Vegas, NV.

[9] Lam, M. S., Rothberg, E. E., and Wolf, M. E. (1991). The cache performance and optimizations of blocked algorithms. In *Proceedings of the Fourth International Conference on Architectural Support for Programming Languages and Operating Systems*, pages 63–74, Santa Clara, CA.

[10] Manjikian, N. and Abdelrahman, T. (1997). Fusion of loops for parallelism and locality. *IEEE Transactions on Parallel and Distributed Systems*, 8(2):193–209.

[11] McKinley, K., Carr, S., and Tseng, C.-W. (1996). Improving data locality with loop transformations. *ACM Transactions on Programming Languages and Systems*, 18(4):424–453.

[12] Mitchell, N., Högstedt, K., Carter, L., and Ferrante, J. (1998). Quantifying the multi-level nature of tiling interactions. *International Journal of Parallel Programming*, 26(6):641–670.

[13] Panda, P., Nakamura, H., Dutt, N., and Nicolau, A. (1999). Augmenting loop tiling with data alignment for improved cache performance. *IEEE Transactions on Computers*, 48(2):142–149.

[14] Park, S. and Miller, K. (1988). Random number generators: Good ones are hard to find. *Communications of the ACM*, 31(10):1192–1201.

[15] Rivera, G. and Tseng, C.-W. (1998). Eliminating conflict misses for high performance architectures. In *Proceedings of the 1998 ACM*

International Conference on Supercomputing, pages 353–360, Melbourne, Australia.

[16] Rivera, G. and Tseng, C.-W. (1999). A comparison of compiler tiling algorithms. In *Proceedings of the Eighth International Conference on Compiler Construction*, Amsterdam, The Netherlands.

[17] Song, Y. and Li, Z. (1999a). A compiler framework for tiling imperfectly-nested loops. In *Proceedings of the Twelfth International Workshop on Languages and Compilers for Parallel Computing*, San Diego, CA.

[18] Song, Y. and Li, Z. (1999b). New tiling techniques to improve cache temporal locality. In *Proceedings of ACM SIGPLAN Conference on Programming Language Design and Implementation*, pages 215–228, Atlanta, GA.

[19] Song, Y. and Li, Z. (2000). Impact of tile-size selection for skewed tiling. Technical Report CSD-TR-00-0018, Department of Computer Science, Purdue University. Also available in http://www.cs.purdue.edu/homes/songyh/academic.html.

[20] Temam, O., Fricker, C., and Jalby, W. (1994). Cache interference phenomena. In *Proceedings of SIGMETRICS'94*, pages 261–271, Santa Clara, CA.

[21] Wolf, M. (1992). *Improving Locality and Parallelism in Nested Loops.* PhD thesis, Department of Computer Science, Stanford University.

[22] Wolf, M. E. and Lam, M. S. (1991). A data locality optimizing algorithm. In *Proceedings of ACM SIGPLAN Conference on Programming Languages Design and Implementation*, pages 30–44, Toronto, Ontario, Canada.

[23] Wolf, M. E., Maydan, D. E., and Chen, D.-K. (1996). Combining loop transformations considering caches and scheduling. In *Proceedings of the Twenty-Ninth Annual IEEE/ACM International Symposium on Microarchitecture*, pages 274–286, Paris, France.

[24] Wolfe, M. (1995). *High Performance Compilers for Parallel Computing.* Addison-Wesley Publishing Company.

Chapter 4

IMPROVING SOFTWARE PIPELINING BY HIDING MEMORY LATENCY WITH COMBINED LOADS AND PREFETCHES

Michael Bedy
Compaq Computer
110 Spit Brook Road (ZKO2-3/N30)
Nashua NH 03062
Michael.Bedy@compaq.com

Steve Carr
Soner Önder
Department of Computer Science
Michigan Technological University
1400 Townsend Dr.
Houghton MI 49931-1295
{carr,soner}@mtu.edu

Philip Sweany
Texas Instruments
P.O Box 660199, MS/8649
Dallas, TX 75266-0199
sweany@ti.com

Abstract Modern processors and compilers hide long memory latencies through non-blocking loads or explicit software prefetching instructions. Unfortunately, each mechanism has potential drawbacks. Non-blocking loads can significantly increase register pressure by extending the lifetimes of loads. Software prefetching increases the number of memory instructions in the loop body. For a loop whose execution time is bound by the number of loads/stores that can be issued per cycle, software prefetching exacerbates this problem and increases the number of idle computational cycles in loops.

In this paper, we show how compiler and architecture support for combining a load and a prefetch into one instruction, called a ***prefetching load***, can give lower register pressure like software prefetching and lower load/store-unit requirements like non-blocking loads. On a set of 106 Fortran loops we show that prefetching loads obtain a speedup of 1.07–1.53 over using just non-blocking loads and a speedup of 1.04–1.08 over using software prefetching. In addition, prefetching loads reduced floating-point register pressure by as much as a factor of 0.4 and integer register pressure by as much as a factor of 0.8 over non-blocking loads. Integer register pressure was also reduced by a factor of 0.97 over software prefetching, while floating-point register pressure was increased by a factor of 1.02 versus software prefetching in the worst case.

Keywords: Cache, Software Prefetching, Nonblocking Loads

1. Introduction

In modern processors, main-memory access time is at least an order of magnitude slower than processor speed. A small, fast cache memory is used to alleviate this problem. However, the cache cannot eliminate all accesses to main memory and programs incur a significant penalty in performance when a miss in the cache occurs. To help tolerate cache miss latency, system designers have developed *non-blocking loads* and *software prefetching* instructions. Non-blocking loads allow cache accesses to continue when misses occur [9], allowing useful work to hide the latency of a cache miss. Software prefetching instructions bring a memory location into the cache in advance of when a load is issued to put the value in a register [12, 21]. Either of these latency hiding techniques can be valuable to the performance of memory systems.

Both of the above latency hiding techniques have disadvantages. Non-blocking loads can increase register pressure in loops significantly by lengthening the lifetimes of loads that are cache misses. Since advanced scheduling techniques such as software pipelining [1] already put a large demand on the register file, the additional pressure due to longer lifetimes can have a detrimental effect on performance. While software prefetching instructions do not increase the register pressure like non-blocking loads, they can cause degradation in loops whose performance is limited by the number of load/store instructions that can be issued per cycle. The additional memory instructions can increase the number of idle computational cycles if there is not a balance between computation and memory instructions.

In this paper, we describe how compilers and architecture can work together to implement *prefetching loads*, a single instruction that performs both a load and prefetch, and detect opportunities for using them effectively. We will show that prefetching loads both enhance the performance and reduce the register pressure of non-blocking load schemes. In addition, we will show that prefetching loads do not require the extra memory instructions required by software prefetching, giving better performance.

This paper begins in Section 2 with background material on memory-reuse analysis and an overview of software pipelining. Then, we give a review of previous work on latency hiding in Section 3. Section 4 compares the differences between non-blocking loads, software prefetching and prefetching loads. Section 5 presents the compiler and hardware support necessary for prefetching loads. Finally, Section 6 details the experimental evaluation of our proposed technique and Section 7 presents our conclusions.

2. Background

In order to utilize prefetching loads, the compiler must perform data-reuse analysis to determine if a prefetching load is profitable and perform software pipelining to schedule the prefetching load. In this section, we present the data-reuse analysis and software pipelining methods that we use in our compilation system.

2.1. Data-Reuse Analysis

Non-blocking loads, software prefetches and prefetching loads all require the compiler to determine which loads and stores will benefit from latency hiding because they are cache misses. Basically the compiler must determine the data reuse properties of each load in a loop.

The two sources of data reuse are *temporal* reuse, multiple accesses to the same memory location, and *spatial* reuse, accesses to nearby memory locations that share a cache line or a block of memory at some level of the memory hierarchy. Temporal and spatial reuse may result from *self-reuse* from a single array reference or *group-reuse* from multiple references.[1] In this paper we use the method developed by Wolf and Lam [27] to determine the reuse properties of loads. An overview of their method follows.

A loop nest of depth n corresponds to a finite convex polyhedron Z^n, called an iteration space, bounded by the loop bounds. Each iteration

[1] Without loss of generality, we assume Fortran's column-major storage.

in the loop corresponds to a node in the polyhedron, and is identified by its index vector $\vec{x} = (x_1, x_2, \ldots, x_n)$, where x_i is the loop index of the ith loop in the nest, counting from the outermost to the innermost. The iterations that can exploit reuse are called the localized iteration space, L. The localized iteration space can be characterized as a localized vector space if the loop bounds are abstracted away.

For example, in the following piece of code, if $L = span\{(1,1)\}$, then data reuse for both A(I) and A(J) is exploited.

```
DO I= 1, N
  DO J = 1, N
    A(I) = A(J) + 2
  ENDDO
ENDDO
```

In Wolf and Lam's model, data reuse can only exist between *uniformly generated* references as defined below [18].

Definition 5 *Let n be the depth of a loop nest, and d be the dimensions of an array* A. *Two references* $A(f(\vec{x}))$ *and* $A(g(\vec{x}))$, *where f and g are indexing functions* $Z^n \rightarrow Z^d$, *are* uniformly generated *if*

$$f(\vec{x}) = H\vec{x} + \vec{c}_f \text{ and } g(\vec{x}) = H\vec{x} + \vec{c}_g$$

where H is a linear transformation and $\vec{c}_f$ *and* $\vec{c}_g$ *are constant vectors.*

For example, in the following loop,

```
DO I= 1, N
  DO J = 1, N
    A(I,J) = A(I,J-1) + A(I+1,J)
  ENDDO
ENDDO
```

the references to A(I,J), A(I,J-1) and A(I+1,J) can be written as

$$\begin{bmatrix} 1 & 0 \\ 0 & 1 \end{bmatrix}\begin{bmatrix} I \\ J \end{bmatrix}+\begin{bmatrix} 0 \\ 0 \end{bmatrix}, \begin{bmatrix} 1 & 0 \\ 0 & 1 \end{bmatrix}\begin{bmatrix} I \\ J \end{bmatrix}+\begin{bmatrix} 0 \\ -1 \end{bmatrix}, \text{ and } \begin{bmatrix} 1 & 0 \\ 0 & 1 \end{bmatrix}\begin{bmatrix} I \\ J \end{bmatrix}+\begin{bmatrix} 1 \\ 0 \end{bmatrix},$$

respectively. References in a loop nest are partitioned into different sets, each of which operates on the same array and has the same H. These sets are called *uniformly generated sets* (UGSs).

A reference is said to have *self-temporal* reuse if $\exists \vec{r} \in L$ such that $H\vec{r} = \vec{0}$. A reference has *self-spatial* reuse if $\exists \vec{r} \in L$ such that $H_S\vec{r} = \vec{0}$, where H_S is H with the first row set to $\vec{0}$. Two distinct references in a

UGS, $\mathtt{A}(H\vec{x} + \vec{c}_1)$ and $\mathtt{A}(H\vec{x} + \vec{c}_2)$ have *group-temporal* reuse if $\exists \vec{r} \in L$ such that $H\vec{r} = \vec{c}_1 - \vec{c}_2$. And finally, two references have *group-spatial* reuse if $\exists \vec{r} \in L$ such that $H_S\vec{r} = \vec{c}_{1,S} - \vec{c}_{2,S}$.

References can be partitioned into groups that have group-temporal reuse called *group-temporal sets* (GTS) and into groups that have group-spatial reuse called *group-spatial sets* (GSS), based upon solving the above equations. Since group-temporal reuse is a special case of group-spatial reuse, a GSS can contain many GTSs. The *leader* of a GSS (GTS) is the first reference to access the cache line (memory location) that is accessed by every array reference in the set. The *leading load* is the first load to access a particular cache line (memory location). Assuming that $L = span\{(0,1)\}$, in the previous example all references belong to the same GSS, `A(I,J)` and `A(I,J-1)` belong to one GTS, and `A(I+1,J)` belongs to another GTS. The leader of the GSS is `A(I+1,J)`.

References that have self-temporal, group-temporal or group-spatial reuse within the localized vector space are said to be cache hits. References that have only self-spatial reuse, are said to be cache misses once every l accesses, where l is the cache-line length, and cache hits otherwise. References that have no reuse are cache misses.

2.2. Software Pipelining

While local and global instruction scheduling can together exploit a large amount of parallelism for non-loop code, exploiting instruction-level parallelism within loops requires software pipelining. Software pipelining can generate efficient schedules for loops by overlapping the execution of operations from different iterations of the loop. This overlapping of operations is analogous to hardware pipelining where speed-up is achieved by overlapping execution of different operations.

Allan et al. [1] provide a good summary of current software pipelining methods, dividing software pipelining techniques into two general categories called *kernel recognition* methods [2, 3, 4] and *modulo scheduling* methods [19, 28, 23]. The software pipelining used in this work is based upon modulo scheduling. Modulo scheduling selects a schedule for one iteration of the loop such that, when that schedule is repeated, no resource or dependence constraints are violated. The number of cycles between the instantiation of successive loop iterations is called the initial interval (*II*). There are two constraints on the *II* of a loop. The first constraint, called the *ResII*, is the maximum number of instructions in a loop requiring a specific functional-unit resource. The second constraint, called the *RecII*, is found by examining the length of recurrences in the data dependence graph (DDG) for a loop. The minimum initiation interval (*MinII*) is the maximum of the *ResII* and *RecII*. In iterative modulo scheduling [23], first a schedule of *MinII* instructions is attempted. If a schedule is found that does not violate any resource or dependence constraints, modulo scheduling has achieved a minimum schedule. If not, scheduling is attempted with *MinII*+ 1 instructions, and then *MinII*+2, ..., continuing up to the worst case which is the *II* is the number of instructions required for local scheduling. The first value of *II* to produce a "legal" schedule of the DDG becomes the actual initiation interval. After a schedule for the loop itself has been found, code to set up the software pipeline (prelude) and drain the pipeline (postlude) are added. Rau [23] provides a detailed discussion of an implementation of modulo scheduling.

2.3. Increased Register Requirements

Software pipelining can, by exploiting inter-iteration concurrency, dramatically reduce the execution time required for a loop. Such overlapping of loop iterations also leads to additional register requirements, however, because the definition and use of a value may span multiple loop iterations. A register may be required for each loop iteration between the definition and use of a value. For example, if a definition and use of a value occurs on the same iteration in a loop one register will suffice for a value. However, if the definition and use of a value are separated by a number of iterations in order to obtain excellent parallelism, a register may be required for every iteration between the definition and use.

3. Previous Work

Callahan, *et al.* [12], describe a simple algorithm for insertion of software prefetches. In one loop iteration, all data needed on the next iteration is prefetched. This simple strategy results in a large percentage of unnecessary prefetches. Some of this overhead can be eliminated by using the *overflow iteration* – the number of loop iterations it takes to fill up the cache – to remove unnecessary prefetches. Any prefetch for an array reference that reuses a value before the overflow iteration occurs is eliminated.

Mowry, *et al.* [21], present an algorithm that outperforms the method of Callahan, *et al.*, by selectively prefetching only those items that are determined to be cache misses by memory reuse analysis. The algorithm also only issues a prefetch for self-spatial references once for each cache line. Additionally, Mowry bases the prefetching distance on the cycle time to memory and the *II* of the loop rather than just prefetching data for the next loop iteration.

Ding, *et al.* [17], report on experiments that show nonblocking loads are an effective way to hide memory latency. They present a simple algorithm that assumes that any reference that has any kind of reuse is always a cache hit. Their study shows that using reuse analysis to determine load latencies is superior to assuming that all loads are cache hits or assuming all loads are cache misses.

Sánchez and González [26] describe a method for scheduling non-blocking loads called Cache Sensitive Modulo Scheduling (CSMS). Their method uses cache reuse analysis (including analysis of cache interferences) to determine whether array references will be cache hits or cache misses. If a load is determined to be a cache miss, but register pressure is estimated to be too high or the load increases the *RecII* of the loop, the load is scheduled as a cache hit. CSMS is shown to give better performance than the algorithm implemented by Ding, *et al.*

Sánchez and González also compare CSMS to software prefetching. However, they do not use full selective prefetching. For array references with self-spatial reuse they issue one prefetch per loop iteration or no prefetches, neither of which is as effective as Mowry's technique. Since prefetches for references with self-spatial reuse are only needed once per cache line, not using full selective prefetching can inhibit the performance of software prefetching. More prefetches are issued than necessary if references with self-spatial reuse are prefetches. Or, fewer prefetches than necessary are issued if no prefetches are issued for references with self-spatial reuse.

Carr and Sweany [15] introduce prefetching loads that only prefetch the next cache line, rather than using a prefetch offset. Their method was limited because prefetching one cache line ahead does not allow enough time to hide miss latency. We improve on this by using a prefetch offset to hide the full miss latency of a load.

4. A Motivating Example for Prefetching Loads

As a comparison of non-blocking loads, software prefetching and prefetching loads, consider the following loop.

```
DO J = 1, N
   DO I = 1, N
       ... = A(I,J) + B(J,I)
   ENDDO
ENDDO
```

Reuse analysis would determine that A(I,J) is a cache miss once out of every l references, where l is the cache-line size. If we issue a non-blocking load using the miss latency, there is needless increase in register pressure due to longer overlapped lifetimes for every $l-1$ out of l references. Note that it is difficult, in general, to determine which of the l references will incur the miss penalty because the alignment of A(I,J) within a cache line may be difficult, or impossible to determine at compile time (*e.g.*, loops in library code).[2] If we assume that A(I,J) is always a cache hit, we keep the register pressure lower, but we pay the cache miss penalty once out of every l references. Neither assumption is adequate for loads with self-spatial reuse. Finally, the reference to B(J,I) would be scheduled as a cache miss, potentially increasing register pressure significantly.

Mowry, *et al.*, would insert an explicit software prefetching instruction once every l iterations of the loop for A(I,J) and an explicit prefetch instruction for B(J,I) every iteration. Assuming that a cache line could hold four elements of A(I,J), Mowry, *et al.*, would unroll the loop by four so that there would be only one prefetch of A(I,J) for each cache line. The resulting loop would have 13 memory operations per 4 floating point operations – worse than the two memory operations per floating point operations in the original loop (Note that loop with prefetching still has better performance because of cache performance improvement). Since modern architectures are often able to issue the same number of floating-point instructions and memory instructions in parallel, the software prefetches would exacerbate the already high demand for issuing memory instructions and leave more computational resources idle than if we could prefetch without additional instructions. So, while the latency could be hidden for all references, the loop would require a longer schedule than if no extra memory instructions were issued.

Our enhancement to latency hiding techniques is to introduce a new instruction, called a *prefetching load*, that is intended for references like A(I,J) and B(J,I) in the example. The instruction is like a normal load except that a prefetching distance is encoded in the offset in register + offset addressing mode or in a special register in register + register addressing mode.[3] The semantics of a prefetching load is to load the data

[2]Our experimentation with scheduling only the first load out of l successive load as a cache miss has shown that only slightly better performance is achieved over assuming that all self-spatial loads are cache hits.

[3]Note that this does not eliminate register + offset mode for references that use prefetching loads. The prefetching load address can be used as the base address for other references to the same cache-line. The reference that uses the prefetching load will be the first reference to a particular cache line, as discussed in the next section.

at the address specified in the address register and prefetch the data at the address in the address register plus the offset (or register). If the prefetching distance is large enough, the part of the instruction that actually loads a value into a register will be a cache hit almost every time.

Prefetching loads can be seen as an enhancement to any non-blocking load scheme since using prefetching loads removes the need to extend register lifetimes like non-blocking loads. Additionally, there is no increase in the number of memory instructions issued like software prefetching. Potentially, prefetching loads can get the best of both non-blocking loads and software prefetching. In the example above, a prefetching load can be issued once every l iterations for `A(I,J)`, using loop unrolling, and once every iteration for `B(J,I)`. This would result in keeping the lower register pressure because all loads, and prefetching loads, can be scheduled using the cache hit latency. Also, this would keep the ratio of memory operations to floating-point operations at two to one, as opposed to the thirteen to four in the loop with software prefetching.

5. Prefetching Loads

In this section, we show how to determine which memory references can benefit from prefetching loads. Then, we describe our cache design.

5.1. Compiler Support for Identifying Candidates for Prefetching Loads

For each GSS that has a constant stride between references, we can issue a prefetching load for the leading load in the GSS. There are two types of GSSs that meet this requirement: (1) a GSS that has self-spatial reuse, or (2) a GSS that has no self reuse, but has the inner-loop induction variable appearing in only one subscript. In case (1), the prefetching load is once every l loop iterations. In case (2), the prefetching load is issued once per loop iteration. If the leading load of a GSS is removed by *scalar replacement* [10, 11], then no prefetching load is issued for that GSS.

As an example, consider the following loop.

```
DO J = 1, N
   DO I = 1, N
      A(I,J) = B(I,J) + B(I-2,J) +
               C(J,I) + C(J,I-1)
   ENDDO
ENDDO
```

In this loop, both `B(I,J)` and `C(J,I)` would be loaded using a prefetching load. Since we need only issue a prefetching load once out of every l references for `B(I,J)`, we unroll the loop by a factor of l and issue the prefetching load for just the original reference.

The prefetch distance is determined by calculating the number of loop iterations that are needed to hide the memory latency. For a software pipelined loop, this is[4]

$$\left\lceil \frac{\text{latency}}{\text{II}} \right\rceil \times \textit{data size}$$

Unfortunately, we cannot be assured of the alignment of a memory reference within the cache line. The alignment may vary on different executions of the loop and invocations of the containing function, or the alignment may not be known at compile time due to separate compilation. This makes it quite difficult to determine which of the l successive references will be hits and which will be misses. For references with self-spatial reuse this can have a significant effect on performance. If the address being prefetched is not aligned on a cache-line boundary, the prefetch will be less effective since a cache miss will still be incurred for a prefetch that is still in flight.

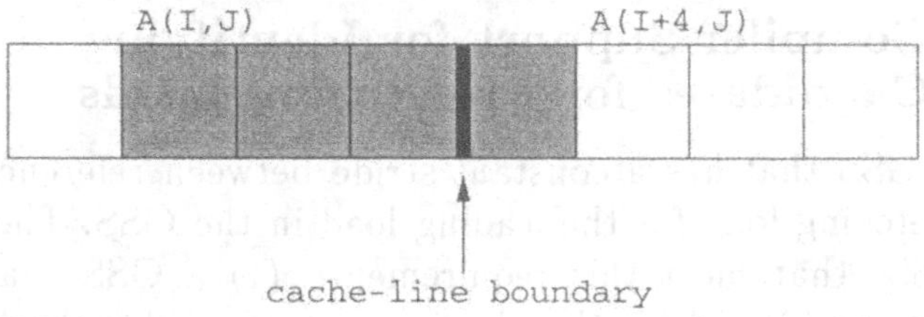

Figure 4.1. Alignment within a Cache Line

Consider prefetching `A(I,J)` from our previous example as shown in Figure 4.1. If we assume that a cache line contains four elements of `A`, it is possible for those four elements to be contained in two cache lines as shown in the shaded area. Thus, a miss to a line whose prefetch has not finished will occur once out of every four references.

To handle this case, we will set the prefetch distance to be one additional cache line ahead of what is computed above, *e.g.*, the line containing `A(I+4,J)`. If we prefetch the line with `A(I+4,J)` enough in advance,

[4] We assume that the stride of self-spatial references is one. This formula can easily be adapted to the case where the stride is greater than one

when A(I,J) is referenced both cache lines in the figure will be present in the cache. Note that the line containing A(I,J) would have been prefetched by an earlier iteration of the loop.

5.2. Cache Design

A prefetching load instruction specifies two memory operations, consisting of the actual load and the prefetching part. In order to handle both parts concurrently, we use a standard two-way interleaved cache to support up to two simultaneous accesses to the cache – one to each module. The MIPS R10000 processor employs such a cache with two banks [20]. The cost of interleaving the cache is the introduction of a multiplexer between the cache and the CPU (Figure 4.2).

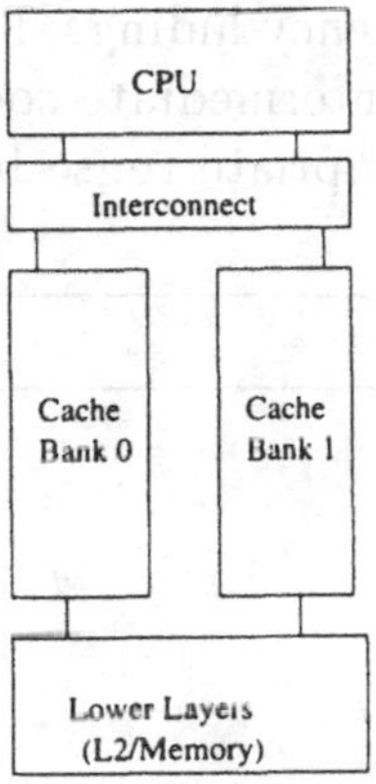

Figure 4.2. Interleaved Cache

In our design, a prefetching load will only proceed if both modules are available. If either cache module is not available, the instruction delays for one cycle and then tries to access both modules again on the next cycle. This continues until both modules can be accessed by the prefetching load. Note that if the prefetch address and the load address access the same cache module, the compiler will increase the prefetch offset by l so that each cache lookup is in a different module. As a result, no delays are encountered because of bank conflicts of the two memory access components of the prefetching load instruction.

An alternative design to replicating the cache port is to allow the load portion of a prefetching load instruction to continue as if it is a regular load instruction and let the prefetching portion take over the cache port in a separate pipeline stage. In such a design, prefetching loads would keep a given cache port for two cycles as opposed to a single cycle utilization for cache hits. Since few prefetching loads are introduced compared to the total number of loads issued, this should not severely effect the performance of regular load instructions. This alternative approach has not been fully explored yet and deserves further study.

6. Experiment

We have implemented non-blocking loads, software prefetching and prefetching loads in our experimental software systems and performed an experiment on 106 loops from the SPEC95 benchmark suite and common kernels. Table 4.1 shows the benchmarks from which the loops come. Memoria, a source-to-source Fortran transformer based upon the D System infrastructure [5], performs the memory reuse analysis and determines which loads need latency hiding. This information is passed on to Rocket [25] via optimized intermediate code [8]. Rocket then software pipelines the code using appropriate reuse-based memory latencies.

Benchmark	*# of Loops*
101.tomcatv	2
102.swim	3
103.su2cor	22
104.hydro2d	38
110.applu	19
125.turb3d	7
141.apsi	3
kernels	11

Table 4.1. Benchmark Loops

Our target architecture for this experiment is a superscalar machine based upon the Unlimited Resource Machine (URM) [22] and has two integer functional units, each with a memory port, and two floating-point functional units. The architecture requires 3 cycles for integer operations and 3 cycles for floating-point operations. The cache for all experiments is as discussed in Section 5.2. We use 16K, 32K, and 64K direct-mapped and two-way set associative caches, each with a 32-byte line size. We use main memory cycle times of 25 and 75 cycles. There is a miss buffer with 16 entries. The architecture assumes that all branches will be taken. Finally, there are 128 integer and 128 floating-point registers. Since our software pipelining implementation does not allow register spilling, a large register set is needed to support scheduling of non-blocking loads.

We have implemented 4 different latency hiding schemes in our software system. Each method uses memory reuse analysis as described in Section 2.1 to determine which memory references are cache hits and which are cache misses. The first scheme (NBLH) uses only a non-blocking load to hide latency and assumes that all array references having any of self-temporal, self-spatial, group-temporal or group-spatial reuse are always cache hits. All other array references are assumed to be cache misses. The second scheme (NBLM) is the same as the first scheme, except that array references that only have self-spatial reuse are assumed to be always a miss. NBLH gives lower register pressure at the cost of performance. NBLM gives better performance at the cost of register pressure.

We have not implemented CSMS for this experiment. The main advantage of CSMS over the simpler methods is its handling of cache misses on recurrences. Prefetching loads could be used as an extension to CSMS also, where we'd expect to see improvements when self-spatial reuse is dominant.

The third scheme tested (Pf) uses software prefetching to hide latency. In this scheme we use full selective prefetching as done by Mowry [21]. Finally, the fourth scheme (Pfld) used for latency hiding is prefetching loads. If an array reference is a cache miss, but is not amenable to prefetching loads (*i.e.*, there is not a constant stride between memory accesses), we issue a non-blocking load using the cache miss latency.

To generate code, we first apply loop unrolling to loops that have array references with only self-spatial reuse. We unroll the loop by the number of array values that fit in a cache line. This allows us to use selective prefetching (and prefetching loads) on references with self-spatial reuse. We perform the unrolling for each latency-hiding scheme so that they each operate on the same code. After unrolling, we perform scalar replacement [13] and then perform memory reuse analysis on the resulting code. We also use array padding for arrays whose dimension sizes cause self interference [24]. The scalar optimizations that we use are constant propagation [29], global value numbering [7], partial redundancy elimination [6], operator strength reduction [16] and dead code elimination. We also generate code using register-plus-offset addressing mode to reduce the integer register pressure and address arithmetic. It is important to note that using register-plus-offset addressing mode is important to the performance of software prefetching. Previous work [14] has shown that the performance of software prefetching is degraded by approximately 20% if proper address arithmetic is not generated. After the code has been optimized, it is then software pipelined using our implementation of Rau's iterative modulo scheduling [23].

6.1. Initiation Interval

Table 4.2 shows the geometric mean increase in *II* for NBLH, NBLM and Pf versus prefetching loads. As predicted, software prefetching has the highest average *II* because of the additional memory operations. Since many loops are bound by memory accesses, adding additional memory operations increases the *ResII* and thus, the *II*. Prefetching loads achieved a slightly lower *II* than both NBLH and NBLM. This is likely due to the change in latencies for some memory operations.

	Memory Latency	
Method	*25 cycles*	*75 cycles*
NBLH	1.01	1.02
NBLM	1.01	1.02
Pf	1.08	1.08

Table 4.2. Geometric Mean Change in II vs. Prefetching Loads

6.2. Performance

Tables 4.3, 4.4 and 4.5 report the geometric mean speedup of prefetching loads over each of the other latency hiding techniques. As expected NBLH performs the worst of the four techniques. Prefetching loads have a geometric mean speedup of 1.24–1.53 over NBLH. Pfld outperforms NBLM by 1.07–1.3.

	Direct-Mapped Cache		2-way Set Associative Cache	
Method	*25 cycles*	*75 cycles*	*25 cycles*	*75 cycles*
NBLH	1.24	1.50	1.24	1.51
NBLM	1.07	1.28	1.08	1.29
Pf	1.04	1.07	1.04	1.06

Table 4.3. Geometric Mean Speedup of Prefetching Loads - 16K Cache

Pfld outperforms software prefetching by a geometric mean speedup of 1.04–1.08. The performance improvement for Pfld is due to the larger achieved *II* for Pf. Pf had a geometric mean increase in instructions executed of a factor of 1.07 at 25 cycles and 1.10 at 75-cycles. The reason for the difference is the change in software pipelining overhead.

In our test cases, Pfld had the best performance on 46% of the loops and tied for the best performance with Pf on 38% of the loops. Pf had

	Direct-Mapped Cache		2-way Set Associative Cache	
Method	*25 cycles*	*75 cycles*	*25 cycles*	*75 cycles*
NBLH	1.24	1.51	1.25	1.50
NBLM	1.09	1.29	1.09	1.29
Pf	1.04	1.07	1.05	1.06

Table 4.4. Geometric Mean Speedup of Prefetching Loads - 32K Cache

	Direct-Mapped Cache		2-way Set Associative Cache	
Method	*25 cycles*	*75 cycles*	*25 cycles*	*75 cycles*
NBLH	1.24	1.51	1.25	1.53
NBLM	1.09	1.29	1.09	1.30
Pf	1.05	1.08	1.05	1.06

Table 4.5. Geometric Mean Speedup of Prefetching Loads - 64K Cache

the best performance on 10% of the loops and one of the non-blocking load schemes performed best on 6% of the loops. Most of the cases where prefetching performed best, it was by a factor of less that 1.02. Some of theses cases can be attributed to higher loop overhead due to differing unroll amounts. In the cases where non-blocking loads performed best, either the loop had too few iterations to benefit from prefetching or there was additional cache interference caused by aggressive prefetching.

6.3. Register Pressure

Table 4.6 shows the geometric mean increase in register pressure versus Pfld. Pfld not only provided better performance than NBLH, NBLM and Pf, but it also required fewer registers. NBLH required a factor of 1.01 more integer registers and a factor of 1.03–1.05 more floating-point registers. NBLM required a factor of 1.10–1.9 more integer registers and a factor of 1.26–2.51 more floating-point registers.

Finally, the register pressure for Pf and Pfld was very close to the same. Pfld had a small decrease in integer register pressure over Pf and a slight increase in floating-point register pressure. This is likely due to the variance in the code generated due to different *II*s being used.

Method	Integer 25 cycles	Integer 75 cycles	Floating Point 25 cycles	Floating Point 75 cycles
NBLH	1.01	1.01	1.03	1.05
NBLM	1.10	1.26	1.9	2.51
Pf	1.03	1.03	0.98	1.02

Table 4.6. Geometric Mean Increase in Register Pressure vs. Prefetching Loads

7. Conclusion

In this paper, we have shown that combining loads and prefetches into one instruction gives better results than non-blocking loads and explicit software prefetches alone. Prefetching loads eliminate the need to extend register lifetimes by scheduling some references as cache misses without increasing the resource requirements of a loop as done with software prefetching. In this way, prefetching loads can get the best features of both non-blocking loads and software prefetching.

Our experiments show a geometric mean speedup of 1.07–1.53 with prefetching loads over using non-blocking loads and a speedup of 1.04–1.08 over software prefetching. Just as importantly, we observed a geometric mean reduction in floating-point register pressure by as much as a factor of 0.4 and a reduction in integer register pressure by as much as a factor of 0.8 versus non-blocking loads. Prefetching loads used a factor of 0.97 fewer integer registers than software prefetching and a factor of 1.02 more floating-point registers in the worst case.

In the future, we will investigate alternate cache designs and other structures to support prefetching loads. The primary goal will be to define a structure that effectively supports that access patterns of prefetching loads.

Given that memory latencies are increasing and that aggressive scheduling techniques such as software pipelining are necessary to get good performance on modern architectures, we need better methods to reduce the negative effects of long latencies. The use of prefetching loads as proposed in this paper is a promising step in alleviating the effects of long latencies for scientific program loops.

Acknowledgments

This research was partially supported by NSF grant CCR-9870871. The authors wish to thank RaeLyn Crowell, Don Darling and Dave

Poplawski for their help in developing the software used in our experiments.

References

[1] V.H. Allan, R. Jones, R. Lee, and S.J. Allan. Software Pipelining. *ACM Computing Surveys*, 27(3), September 1995.

[2] A. Aiken and A. Nicolau. Optimal loop parallelization. In *Conference on Programming Language Design and Implementation*, pages 308–317, Atlanta Georgia, June 1988. SIGPLAN '88.

[3] A. Aiken and A. Nicolau. Perfect Pipelining: A New Loop Optimization Technique. In *Proceedings of the 1988 European Symposium on Programming, Springer Verlag Lecture Notes in Computer Science, #300*, pages 221–235, Nancy, France, March 1988.

[4] V.H. Allan, M. Rajagopalan, and R.M. Lee. Software Pipelining: Petri Net Pacemaker. In *Working Conference on Architectures and Compilation Techniques for Fine and Medium Grain Parallelism*, Orlando, FL, January 20-22 1993.

[5] V. Adve, J-C. Wang, J. Mellor-Crummey, D. Reed, M. Anderson, and K. Kennedy. An integrated compilation and performance analysis environment for data parallel programs. In *Proceedings of Supercomputing '95*, San Diego, CA, December 1995.

[6] Preston Briggs and Keith D. Cooper. Effective partial redundancy elimination. In *Proceedings of the ACM SIGPLAN '94 Conference on Programming Language Design and Implementation*, pages 159–170, Orlando, FL, June 1994.

[7] P. Briggs, K. D. Cooper, and L. T. Simpson. Value numbering. *Software - Practice & Experience*, 27(6):701–724, June 1997.

[8] Preston Briggs. The massively scalar compiler project. Technical report, Rice Univeristy, July 1994. Preliminary version available via anonymous ftp.

[9] Tien-Fu Chen and Jean-Loup Baer. Reducing memory latency via non-blocking and prefetching caches. In *Proceedings of the Fifth International Conference on Architectural Support for Programming Languages and Operating Systems*, pages 51–61, Boston, Massachusetts, 1992.

[10] David Callahan, Steve Carr, and Ken Kennedy. Improving register allocation for subscripted variables. In *Proceedings of the ACM SIGPLAN '90 Conference on Programming Language Design and Implementation*, pages 53–65, White Plains, NY, June 1990.

[11] S. Carr and K. Kennedy. Scalar replacement in the presence of conditional control flow. *Software Practice and Experience*, 24(1):51–77, January 1994.

[12] David Callahan, Ken Kennedy, and Allan Porterfield. Software prefetching. In *Proceedings of the Fourth International Conference on Architectural Support for Programming Languages and Operating Systems*, pages 40–52, Santa Clara, California, 1991.

[13] Steve Carr, Kathryn McKinley, and Chau-Wen Tseng. Compiler optimizations for improving data locality. In *Proceedings of the Sixth International Conference on Architectural Support for Programming Languages and Operating Systems*, pages 252–262, Santa Clara, California, 1994.

[14] R. Crowell. An experimental evaluation of compiler-based cache management techniques. Master's thesis, Michigan Technological University, March 1998.

[15] S. Carr and P. Sweany. Improving software pipelining with hardware support for self-spatial loads. In *The Third Workshop on Interaction between Compilers and Computer Architecture (INTERACT-3)*, San Jose, CA, October 1998.

[16] Keith D. Cooper, L. Taylor Simpson, and Christopher A. Vick. Operator strength reduction. Technical Report CRPC-TR95635-S, Center for Research on Parallel Computation, Rice Univeristy, October 1995.

[17] C. Ding, S. Carr, and P. Sweany. Modulo scheduling with cache reuse information. In *Proceedings of EuroPar '97*, Passau, Germany, August 1997.

[18] D. Gannon, W. Jalby, and K. Gallivan. Strategies for cache and local memory management by global program transformations. In *Proceedings of the First International Conference on Supercomputing*. Springer-Verlag, Athens, Greece, 1987.

[19] Monica Lam. Software pipelining: An effective scheduling technique for VLIW machines. In *Proceedings of the ACM SIGPLAN '88 Conference on Programming Language Design and Implementation*, pages 318–328, Atlanta, GA, July 1988.

[20] MIPS Technologies, Incorporated. *R10000 Microprocessor Product Overview*, October 1994.

[21] Todd C. Mowry, Monica S. Lam, and Anoop Gupta. Design and evaluation of a compiler algorithm for prefetching. In *Proceedings of the Fifth International Conference on Architectural Support for Pro-*

gramming Languages and Operating Systems, pages 62–75, Boston, Massachusetts, 1992.

[22] D.A. Poplawski. The unlimited resource machine (URM). Technical Report 95-01, Michigan Technological University, January 1995.

[23] B. R. Rau. Iterative modulo scheduling: An algorithm for software pipelining loops. In *Proceedings of the 27th International Symposium on Microarchitecture (MICRO-27)*, pages 63–74, San Jose, CA, December 1994.

[24] G. Rivera and C.-W. Tseng. Data transformations for eliminationg conflict misses. In *Proceedings of the 1998 ACM SIGPLAN Conference on Programming Language Design and Implementation*, pages 38–49, Montreal, Canada, June 17-19 1998.

[25] Philip H. Sweany and Steven J. Beaty. Overview of the Rocket retargetable C compiler. Technical Report CS-94-01, Department of Computer Science, Michigan Technological University, Houghton, January 1994.

[26] F. Sánchez and A. González. Cache-sensitive modulo scheduling. In *Proceedings of the 30th International Symposium on Microarchitecture (MICRO-30)*, Research Triangle Park, NC, December 1997.

[27] Michael E. Wolf and Monica S. Lam. A data locality optimizing algorithm. In *Proceedings of the ACM SIGPLAN '91 Conference on Programming Language Design and Implementation*, pages 30–44, Toronto, Ontario, June 1991.

[28] Nancy J. Warter, Scott A. Mahlke, W.-M. Hwu, and B. Ramakrishna Rau. Reverse if-conversion. In *Proceedings of the ACM SIGPLAN '93 Conference on Programming Language Design and Implementation*, pages 290–299, Albuquerque, NM, June 1993.

[29] Mark N. Wegman and F. Kenneth Zadeck. Constant propagation with conditional branches. *ACM Transactions on Programming Languages and Systems*, 13(2):181–210, April 1991.

Chapter 5

REGISTER ALLOCATION FOR EMBEDDED SYSTEM IN THE PRESENCE OF JAVA EXCEPTION

Heung-Bok Lee
Seoul National University, Korea
darong@altair.snu.ac.kr

Byung-Sun Yang
Seoul National University, Korea
scdoner@altair.snu.ac.kr

Soo-Mook Moon
Seoul National University, Korea
smoon@altair.snu.ac.kr

Abstract In Java, an exception thrown in a `try` block can be handled in one of `catch` blocks given by the programmer. On exception, local variables must be preserved to be usable in the `catch` block, while operand stack is flushed. This error handling mechanism raises an interesting challenge, called *local variable consistency problem*, in implementing register allocation during JIT compilation. Because the register allocation for local variables should be consistent between a possibly exception generatable instruction (PEI) in a `try` block and `catch` blocks.

In the viewpoint of register allocation, there are two approaches to solve the problem introduced in the literature in JIT compilation techniques. One is to allocate a local variable to a fixed location, which leads to simple implementation with little memory overhead. The other is to allocate a local variable to variable locations in a flexible way for better performance, while sacrificing more memory to store local variable mapping information at each PEI.

In this paper, we introduce another solution, called *partially fixed register allocation*, to the problem. The register allocator allocates a local variable to a fixed location only in `try` blocks, with a flexible allocation in other parts of a method.

Experiments on the ARM platform with SPECjvm98 benchmarks reveal that our approach requires almost the same memory as the previous fixing register allocation with little performance degradation compared to the flexible register allocation. We expect that this approach illuminates a good engineering solution for JIT compilers in embedded systems with limited memory.

Keywords: Exception handling, Register allocation, Just-in-time compilation, Embedded System.

1. Introduction

Recently, Java system becomes a promising execution environment for embedded systems as well as desktop and server systems. One of the reasons for its success is robustness, which can be achieved through exception handling, a language feature supported by Java.

Unlike traditional programming languages such as C, Java makes it possible to cope with unexpected errors in a clean and safe way at runtime by using try/catch/finally blocks, program constructs for exception handling. An exception thrown in a try block can be handled in one of catch blocks associated with the try block. After this, codes specified in a finally block will be executed regardless of generation of the exception.

However, this useful language feature raises an interesting issue, called *local variable consistency problem*, in the design of a JIT compiler, a performance-delivering JVM component. According to the Java VM specification [10], local variables defined in the normal flow of a method can be used in catch blocks. Thus, register allocation for local variables must be consistent between a try block and catch blocks associated with the block.

An interpreter usually uses a predetermined memory location for a local variable, so that the allocation consistency requirement is satisfied without any efforts. Whereas, an optimizing JIT compiler, which may allocate local variables to different memory locations or registers, must be aware of this consistency requirement. The register allocation results for local variables at all possible exception generatable instructions(PEI) [8] in a try block should be propagated to associated catch blocks for register allocation for the associated catch blocks.

As far as we know, there are two approaches to deal with the consistency issue in existing JIT compilers. One is to allocate a local variable to a predetermined location.[6, 7, 9] Since local variables are allocated to fixed locations, the allocation becomes consistent between a try block and the associated catch blocks like the case of an interpreter. This approach makes the implementation of register allocation simple, while the fixed allocation for local variables may lead to poor-quality code.

The other is to allocate local variables flexibly as normal, ignoring the existence of catch blocks.[4] The consistency can be accomplished by keeping the register allocation result for local variables at every PEI in a try block. The JIT compiler can use the allocation map for translation of catch blocks.[1] This allocation flexibility gives better-quality code, with sacrificing memory for storing allocation results. And this memory overhead can be a problem in embedded systems.

In this paper, we introduce a new efficient approach for the local variable consistency problem, a reasonable trade-off between memory overhead and performance, which is attractive to embedded systems. Like the first approach above, our approach allocates local variables to fixed locations. However, we fix local variables only in try blocks and perform an aggressive register allocation for other normal regions and methods without catch blocks. To fix a local variable in a try block, the allocator makes a local variable not to be coalesced with other local variables, while it does not block a local variable to be coalesced with other non-local variables. So we can expect better code than that of the first approach. And because of the same local variable map at all PEIs in a try block, no additional memory is required to remember local variable map. Our experiment reveals that the performance degradation of new approach is acceptable for embedded system when we compare it with flexible allocation approach.

The rest of this paper is organized as follows. Section 2 reviews Java exception mechanism and the local variable consistency problem. We describe how to fix local variable map in our register allocation algorithm in Section 3. Section 4 shows experimental results. And the summary of this paper appears in Section 5.

2. Java exception and local variable consistency problem

Java uses *exceptions* to provide elegant error handling capabilities during program execution.[5] A Java exception can be generated by a JVM when a runtime error such as `OutOfMemoryError` occurs, or thrown through an explicit `throw` statement by the Java program. A program-

[1] Translation of catch blocks can be delayed to the time they are actually used to handle a thrown exception as in LaTTe[?].

mer can mark an exception-prone code segment as a `try` block, and provide several `catch` blocks in order to handle exceptions raised in the `try` block.

When an exception occurs, program control is transfered from the exception point in a `try` block to one of the `catch` blocks associated with it. If there is no `catch` block to handle the exception in the method where the exception is thrown, the method is terminated abnormally and the JVM searches backward through the method call stack to the find a `catch` block that can handle the exception.[10]

According to the JVM specification, the JVM should recover program context, specifically local variables, at the exception point when transferring control to a `catch` block. Instead, the operand stack is flushed and a reference to the exception is pushed onto the stack. In more detail, if the catch block is found in the method where the exception has been raised, the JVM should recover local variables at the exception point. If the catch block is found in another method which is on the call chain to the method where exception raised, the JVM should recover local variables at the call instruction to the call chain.

An interpreter usually uses a fixed memory location for a local variable, which means that the local variable map is always identical at every PEI.[9, 2] Therefore, the local variable recovery is simple. In contrast, a JIT compiler may allocate various memory locations, registers or stack memory, to a local variable at different program points. This allocation flexibility raises an issue, called *local variable consistency problem*, to the JIT compiler. For correct local variable recovery, the JIT compiler has to either perform register allocation consistent between an exception point and the catch block handling the exception or provide allocation information to the JVM for bookkeeping. This problem requests the JIT compiler a carefully treatment for each PEI during register allocation.

From the literature on the Java JIT compilation, we found that solutions to the local variable consistency problem can be classified into two categories in the viewpoint of register allocation at PEIs[2];

- to allocate a predetermined location, i.e., a fixed register or a fixed stack area, to a local variable, or

- to perform a flexible register allocation for local variables without considering exception points.

[2]There are only a few papers which explicitly take the problem into consideration when introducing their register allocation mechanism. So this categorization is based on our own interpretation of the techniques.

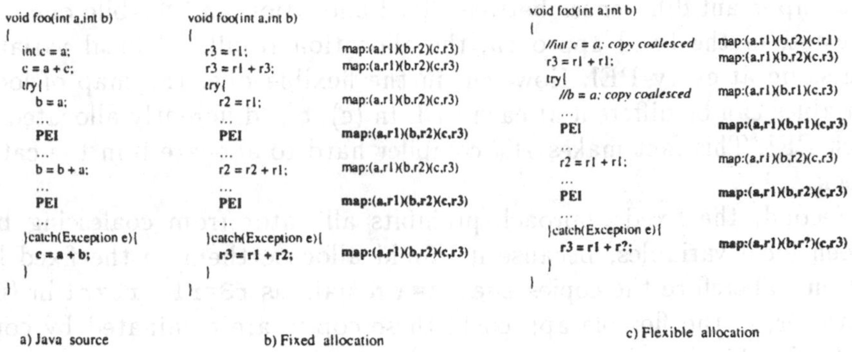

Figure 5.1. Register allocation examples of fixed allocation and flexible allocation

In the first approach, the JIT compiler allocates a fixed memory location to a local variable. It reserves several registers and stack area for local variables and fixes the allocation for local variables in the whole method. For catch blocks, the register allocator uses the fixed local variable map. Consequently, the local variable allocation becomes consistent between a try block and catch blocks, allowing that program control can be transferred easily. This approach makes it easy to implement the JIT compilation in presence of exceptions, but taints code quality in a normal flow resulting in peformace degradation. Local variables cannot be coalesced with one another.

The second approach is to allocate local variables flexibly at PEIs. The JIT compiler ignores the presence of exception for allocation for a try block. Since local variable maps can be different between PEIs, they must be remembered at all PEIs for correct register allocation for catch blocks.[3] LaTTe[4] deploys this approach. It generates local variable map tables at all PEIs during translation of the normal flow of a method. On an exception, LaTTe translates the catch block with the local variable map at the exception point.

Since it does not affect the code quality in the normal flow, its performance will be better than that of the first approach. However it requires additional information to remember local variable map, which makes it hard to use the approach in embedded systems with tight memory constraint.

[3]The map information may be represented with an explicit map table or a sequence of copies between a PEI and catch blocks.

Figure 5.1 compares the two register allocation approaches. It shows two important differences between fixed allocation and flexbile one.

First, in the fixed approach, the allocation results of local variable are same at every PEI. However, in the flexible one, the map of local variables can be different at each PEI. In (c), `b` is differently allocated at each PEI. This fact makes JIT compiler hard to allocate `b` in the catch block.

Second, the fixed approach prohibits allocator from coalescing between local variables, because it should allocate them to the fixed location. Therefore the copies `c=a, b=a` remain as `r3=r1, r2=r1` in (b). However, in the flexible approach, these copies are eliminated by copy coalescing like in (c).

3. Partially fixed register allocation algorithm

In this section, we describe our approach for the local variable consistency problem. In brief, the JIT compiler fixes local variables only at PEIs in try blocks while allocating local variables flexibly for other parts of a method and methods without catch blocks.

```
void foo(int a,int b)
{
    int c = a;
    c = a + c;
    try{
      b = a;
      ...
      PEI
      ...
      b = b + a;
      ...
      PEI
      ...
    }catch(Exception e){
      c = a + b;
    }
}
```

a) Java source

```
void foo(int a,int b)
{
    //int c = a; copy coalesced    map:(a,r1)(b,r2)(c,r1)
    r3 = r1 + r1;                  map:(a,r1)(b,r2)(c,r3)
    try{
      r2 = r1;                     map:(a,r1)(b,r2)(c,r3)
      ...
      PEI                          map:(a,r1)(b,r2)(c,r3)
      ...
      r2 = r1 + r1;                map:(a,r1)(b,r2)(c,r3)
      ...
      PEI                          map:(a,r1)(b,r2)(c,r3)
      ...
    }catch(Exception e){
      r3 = r1 + r2;                map:(a,r1)(b,r2)(c,r3)
    }
}
```

b) Partially fixed allocation

Figure 5.2. Register allocation example of partially fixed allocation

Our register allocation algorithm is a lightweight version of what is used by LaTTe[4] tailored for embedded systems. The algorithm is local, whose allocation unit is a *basic block*. During register allocation, a copy corresponding to `push` or `pop` is coalesced by mapping its source and destination onto the same register. The register allocation for each instruction is comprised of three stages; 1)copy coalescing, 2)source allocation, and 3)destination allocation.

copy coalescing The allocator coalesces all kinds of copies (local/stack, stack/stack, local/local) for copy elimination. In a try block, it does not coalesce a copy between local variables.

source allocation Normally, a source variable has been already allocated to a register during destination allocation for a previous instruction. If a source variable has been spilled, however, it is allocated to a new free register with changing the local variable map. In a try block, a spilled local variable is *copied* to a scratch register *without* changing the local variable map. The scratch register is used for execution of the instruction.

destination allocation A destination variable is allocated to a free register. In a try block, if a local variable has been coalesced with other variables, the other variables are splitted by adding a copy with preserving the the local variable map. And, like the source allocation, a spilled local variable is *copied* to a scratch register without modification of the local variable map.

Actually, each stage has two modes; *flexible* and *fixed* mode. The flexible mode is for register allocation in normal parts of a method, while the fixed mode is for register allocation in try blocks.

In the flexible mode, the register allocation is almost similar to the `forward sweep` [4] in LaTTe. Copies between variables are aggressively eliminated through coalescing. So that the allocation result of a local variable may be changed when the variable is newly defined by an instruction, or when the variable is spilled and when the spilled variable is about to be used by an instruction.

In the fixed mode, all local variables are allocated to their fixed memory locations (registers and stack memory), which are distinct to one another.[4] The register allocator prohibits a local variable from being coalesced with other local variables. The local variable map is not changed at all. If a local variable is mapped to a memory by spilling, it is copied to a scratch register for the temporary use of an instruction.

Figure 5.2 illustrates the register allocation for the same example in Figure 5.1. The first copy `c=a` outside the try block is removed by copy coalescing. On the while, the second copy `b=a` in the try block remains

[4]Before entering a try block, the register allocator splits coalesced local variables to their own predetermined locations.

because a is fixed to r1 and b is fixed to r2 in the block. Since the allocation result of local variables is same at every PEI, the catch block can be translated easily with the same local variable map in the try block.

4. Experimental result

This section presents an empirical comparison of the performance between the three approaches for the local variable consistency problem; *fixed*, *flexible*, *partially fixed* allocation. For the performance evaluation, we measured the runtime counts of copy and spill, and the running time of benchmark programs.

SPECjvm98[3] was used as benchmark programs. But the implemenation of exception handling in flexible allocation is not finished, so we exculde the programs, _228_jack and _213_javac, that raise exceptions at runtime in benchmark. And for the same reason, we didn't measured memory overhead of flex allocation.

SPECjvm98 might not be perfectly adequate as benchmark for embedded systems because it has been designed for desktop systems running client Java programs. However, there is no standard Java benchmark set for embedded systems.

For the experiment, *pLaTTe*, a Java JIT compiler for embedded system, was used. pLaTTe is a lightweight version of LaTTe. It targets high-end embedded systems such as Web phone and Digital TV. The memory capacity of these high-end embedded system will be in the range from 16MB to 32MB and their CPU will be a 32-bit micro-controller with clock cycle between 100Mhz and 200Mhz. The runtime memory permitted to the JIT compiler is about from 500K to 2M. So, reducing memory overhead is very important issue. The static image size of pLaTTe is about 120K and the size of JITed code is three to five times larger than Java bytecode size. Our experiments was performed on the ARM based PC, Netwinder [1], equipped with StrongARM110 275Mhz and 64MB memory, running Linux.

In order to evaluate the performance of our approach, we compared the runtime counts of copy and spill(load+store). This result was produced by running SPECjvm98 with -s10. Figure 5.3 shows the performance difference between partially fixed allocation and fixed allocation.

It shows that there is little performance difference between partially fixed allocation and flexible one. However, in the figure 5.4, the difference between partially fixed allocation and fixed one is not small. For _202_jess, the load/store count of partially fixed allocation is 40% that of fixed one. On the other hand ,in _227_mtrt, the spill count of fixed allocation is smaller than that of partially fixed allocation.

However, Figure 5.1 shows the effect is not high in real time. The overall performace enhancement of flexible allocation to the fixed allocation is less than 1 percentage. One of the reasons is that it is not well tuned, so the effect of flexible allocation is not shown well. But we found that there are other important reasons.

According to our analysis, there are two main reasons that sometimes the fixed allocation has better performance than others unexpectedly. One is due to inefficient compilation for some large methods, which might be used rarely in the embedded system. In the flexible allocation and the partially fixed one, the aggressive coalescing increased register pressure, so it generated more spill codes. The other reason is that flexible allocation tends to generate many copies at join points in case of large methods having complex control flows. Since the current implementation traverses basic blocks in DFS order to do one pass allocation[5], all coalesced variables are splitted at join points. It generates additional copies that may not be done in the fixed allocation. Becasue in fixed allocation, probability of allocation conflict at join points is lower than that of the flexible one.

Table 5.1. Runtime result for the SPECjvm98

Benchmark	fixed	flexible	partial	flex/part	fix/part
_201_compress	24.69	24.51	24.59	0.992	0.995
_202_jess	8.93	8.85	9.15	0.991	1.024
_209_db	6.22	6.19	6.40	0.995	1.028
_222_mpegaudio	676.29	675.83	676.79	0.999	1.000
_227_mtrt	92.74	92.40	92.61	0.996	0.998

5. Summary

In this paper, we described our new approach for the local variable consistency problem. Our approach is to fix the local variable allocation at PEIs only in try blocks and to allocate flexibly a variable in other region. In order to fix the local variable allocation, the register allocator prohibits coalescing between local variables, while allowing a local variable to be coalesced with other non-local variables. The partially fixed register allocation reduces performance degradation caused by fixing lo-

[5]LaTTe traverses basic blocks in reverse post order to minimize copies at join point

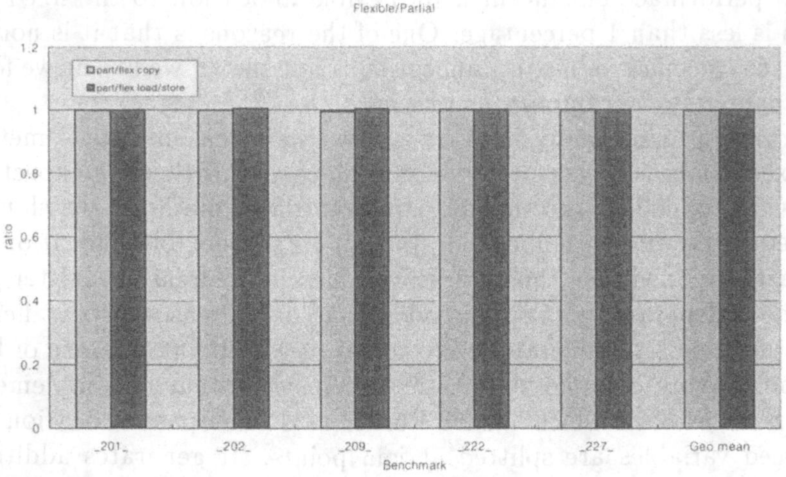

Figure 5.3. Runtime copy and spill count ratio between flexible allocation and partially fixed allocation for SPECjvm98

cal variables. And there is little additional memory overhead because the local variable map does not have to be remembered as in the flexible register allocation. However, experiment results show that the performance gap is just small between flexible allocation and fixed allocation. And the main reason is that the agressive copy coalescing with few registers cause more spill codes. So we expect the performace effect of partially fixed allocation will be shown on the system that has sufficient registers not to spill many variables like MIPS cpu whose registers are 32.

References

[1] NetWinder OfficeServer. http://www.netwinder.org.

[2] (1998). JDK 1.1.6 Production Release for Solaris. http://www.sun.com/solaris/java.

[3] (1998). SPEC JVM98 Benchmarks. http://www.spec.org/osg/jvm98.

[4] Ebcioğlu,, B.-S. Y. S.-M. M. . S. P. J. L. S. L. J. P. . Y. C. . S. K. K.

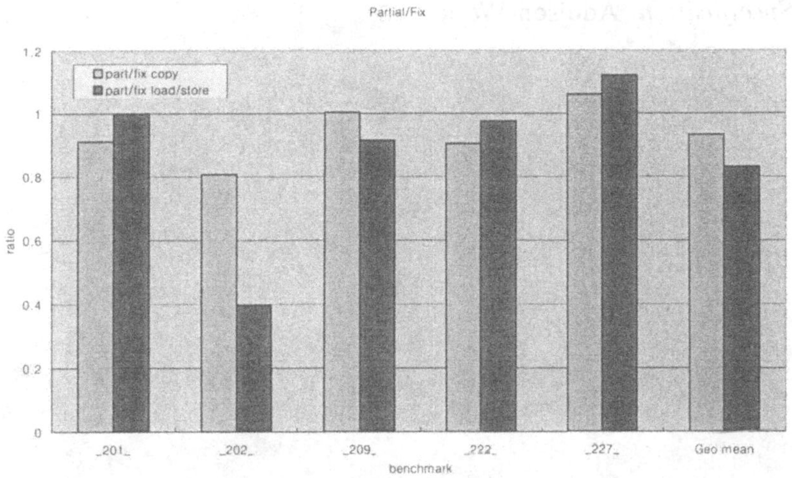

Figure 5.4. Runtime copy, load/store count ratio between fixed allocation and partially fixed allocation for SPECjvm98

and Altman, E. (Oct 1999). Efficient Java Exception Handling in Just-in-Time Compilation. In *The 1999 International Conference on Parallel Architectures and Compilation Technique.*

[5] Joy,, G. G. B. and Steele, G. (1997). *The Java Language Specification.* Addison-Wesley.

[6] Krall, A. and Grafl, R. (1997). Cacao - A 64-Bit Java VM Just-in-Time Compiler. In *PPoPP '97 Workshop on Java for Science and Engineering Compuation.*

[7] Parikh,, A.-R. A.-T. M. C. G.-Y. L. V. M. and Stichnoth, J. M. (Jun 1998). Fast, Effective Code Generation in a Just-In-Time Java Compiler. In *The ACM SIGPLAN'98 Conference on Programming Language Design and Implementation.*

[8] Sarkar, J. C. D. G. M. H. V. (Sept 1999). Efficient and Precise Modeling of Exceptions for the Analysis of Java Programs. In *The 1999 ACM SIGPLAN-SIGSOFT Workshop on Program Analysis for Software Tools and Enginerring.*

[9] Wilkinson, T. (1998). Kaffe: A JIT and Interpreting Virtual Machine to Run Java Code. http://www.transvirtual.com/.

[10] Yellin, F. and Lindholm, T. (1996). *The Java Virtual Machine Specification.* Addison-Wesley.

Chapter 6

IS COMPILING FOR PERFORMANCE == COMPILING FOR POWER?

Madhavi Valluri and Lizy K. John
Laboratory for Computer Architecture
The University of Texas at Austin
{valluri,ljohn}@ece.utexas.edu

Abstract Energy consumption and power dissipation are increasingly becoming important design constraints in high performance microprocessors. Compilers traditionally are not exposed to the energy details of the processor. However, with the increasing power/energy problem, it is important to evaluate how the existing compiler optimizations influence energy consumption and power dissipation in the processor. In this chapter we present a quantitative study wherein we examine the effect of the standard optimizations levels -O1 to -O4 of DEC Alpha's *cc* compiler on power and energy of the processor. We also evaluate the effect of four individual optimizations on power/energy and attempt to classify them as "low energy" or "low power" optimizations. In our experiments we find that optimizations that improve performance by reducing the number of instructions are optimized for energy. Such optimizations reduce the total amount of work done by the program. This is in contrast to optimizations that improve performance by increasing the overlap in the program during execution. The latter kind of optimizations increase the average power dissipated in the processor.

1. Introduction

Energy consumption and power dissipation are increasingly becoming important design constraints in high performance microprocessors. Power dissipation affects circuit reliability and packaging costs. Energy consumption directly affects battery life. With the increasing use of general purpose processors in the embedded world, designing low energy processors is important. Gowan et al. [5], discuss the power and energy trends of three generations of Alpha processors. Power dissipation increases significantly from one generation to the next despite the reduced supply voltages and advanced processor technologies. The paper shows the power in the Alpha 21264 increasing almost linearly with frequency, with power reaching 72 Watts at 600MHz. The maximum power dissipated under worst case conditions was found to be about 95 Watts. These examples clearly indicate that power dissipation and energy consumption will soon become important limiting factors in the design of high performance processors.

Until recently, the two problems were being dealt with only at the circuit-level. Voltage scaling, low swing buses, conditional clocking etc have helped alleviate the problems enormously. However, architectural-level and compiler-level analysis can help tackle these problems much earlier in the design cycle. Recently, several architectural and compiler techniques have been proposed to reduce power and energy [3, 6, 7, 8, 9, 10, 11, 12]. In our work we concentrate on the influence of compilers on power dissipation and energy consumption.

Compilers traditionally are not exposed to the energy details of the processor. Current compiler optimizations are tuned primarily for performance and occasionally for code size. With the increasing power/energy problem, it is important to evaluate how the existing optimizations influence energy consumption and power dissipation in the processor. An interesting question to answer would be - if we compile for performance, are we automatically compiling for low power or low energy? Current compilers already have two axes in the optimizations used - namely compiling for speed (in general-purpose processors) and compiling for code size (in embedded systems), do we need a third axis with optimizations that *compile for power/energy*?

To answer the above questions, we present a quantitative study wherein we examine the influence of a few state-of-the-art compiler optimizations on energy and power of the complete processor. We study the effect of the standard optimizations levels `-O1` to `-O4` of DEC Alpha's *cc* compiler on power and energy of the processor. We also evaluate the effect of four individual optimizations on power/energy and attempt to classify them as "low energy optimizations" or "low power optimizations" or both. The optimizations we study are *simple basic-block scheduling, loop unrolling, function inlining, and aggressive global scheduling.* For our experiments, we use Wattch [2], an architectural simulator that estimates CPU energy consumption. Wattch integrates parameterizable power models into the *Simplescalar* [4] processor simulator.

In our study we find that the set of compiler optimizations that improve performance by reducing the number of instructions executed are optimized for both energy and power. This is in contrast to optimizations that improve performance by increasing the existing parallelism in the program. The latter kind of optimizations increase the average power dissipated in the processor. We find that optimizations such as common-subexpression elimination, copy propagation, loop unrolling are very good for reducing energy since they reduce the number of instructions in the program, hence the amount of total work done is less in programs with these optimizations. Such optimizations should definitely be included in the *compile for power/energy* switch. Optimizations such as instruction scheduling significantly increase power (and may occasionally increase energy) because they increase the overlap in programs without reducing the total number of instructions in the program. However, such optimizations can be easily modified to take power details into consideration and can be used to increase performance without increasing average power.

The rest of the chapter is organized as follows: In Section 2 we discuss some previous work that has been done in the area of compilers and low power/energy. Section 3 shows a few examples that motivates the need for our study. We describe the different compiler optimizations evaluated in Section 4. In Section 5 we describe our experimental framework and discuss in detail the results obtained. Finally, we provide concluding remarks and future directions in Section 6.

2. Related Work

In this section we present some of the previous work done in understanding the interaction between the compiler and power/energy of the processor.

The study by Kandemir et al. [7] quantitatively examines the influence of different high-level compiler optimizations on system energy. However, in their study, they evaluate only loop-nest optimizations such as loop fusion, loop fission, blocking, tiling, scalar expansion and unrolling. In our study, we discuss both the power dissipated and energy consumption details, while in the paper by Kandemir et al., they report only energy details. Their main observation in the paper is that the optimizations appear to increase the energy consumed in the core while reducing the energy consumed in the memory system. Unoptimized codes consume more energy in the memory system.

There have been a few instruction scheduling techniques proposed which attempt to reduce the power dissipated in the processor. Su et al. [11] proposed *cold scheduling*, wherein, they assign priority to instructions based on some pre-determined power cost and use a generic list scheduler to schedule the instructions. The power cost of scheduling an instruction depends on the instruction it is being scheduled after. This corresponds to the switching activity on the control path. Toburen et al. [12] propose another power-aware scheduler which schedules as many instructions as possible in a given cycle until the energy threshold of that cycle is reached. Once that precomputed threshold is reached, scheduling proceeds to the next time-step or cycle. In our work, by evaluating several state-of-the-art optimizations, we attempt to identify other optimizations besides instruction scheduling that can be improved if the power/energy models of the processor were exposed to them.

Significant work has been done in reducing energy consumption in the memory. Most techniques achieve a reduction in energy through innovative architectural techniques [6, 8, 9, 10]. Some of the works that include compiler involvement are [6] and [10]. In [6], the authors suggest the use of an L-cache. An L-cache is a small cache which is placed between the I-cache and CPU. The L-cache is very small (holds a few basic blocks), hence consumes less energy. The compiler is used to select good basic blocks to place in the L-cache. Another approach to reduce memory energy is Gray code addressing [10]. This form of addressing reduces the bit switching activity in the instruction address path. Bunda et al. [3] and Asanovic [1] investigated the effect of energy-aware instruction sets. These techniques would involve the compiler even earlier in the code generation process. The paper by Bunda et al [3] concentrates on reducing memory energy, and Asanovic [1] investigates new instructions to reduce energy in the memory, register files and pipeline stages.

3. Motivating Examples

Consider the data dependence graph (DDG) shown in Figure 6.1(b). It contains six operations. All operations except `op E` have a latency of one cycle, `op E` takes two cycles to complete. We will assume there are infinite functional units for this example. An instruction scheduler that attempts to also optimize for registers would schedule `op E` as close to `op F` as possible. The resulting schedule can be seen in Figure 6.1(b). If we assume that each operation consumes one unit of power, compared to the schedule in Figure 6.1(b), the schedule in Figure 6.1(c), dissipates less peak power (3 units vs 2 units in Figure 6.1(b)). Figure 6.1(c) is also a valid schedule. By extending the lifetime of `op E` by one cycle, we reduce the peak power dissipated without affecting performance. The design choice of letting `op E` occupy the register for one cycle longer than required will prove to be inexpensive only if there are sufficient number of registers. Current schedulers do not take power details into consideration and hence might schedule `op E` in cycle 2 even if there are sufficient registers. This example shows that two variations of the same code can have the same performance but different power requirements.

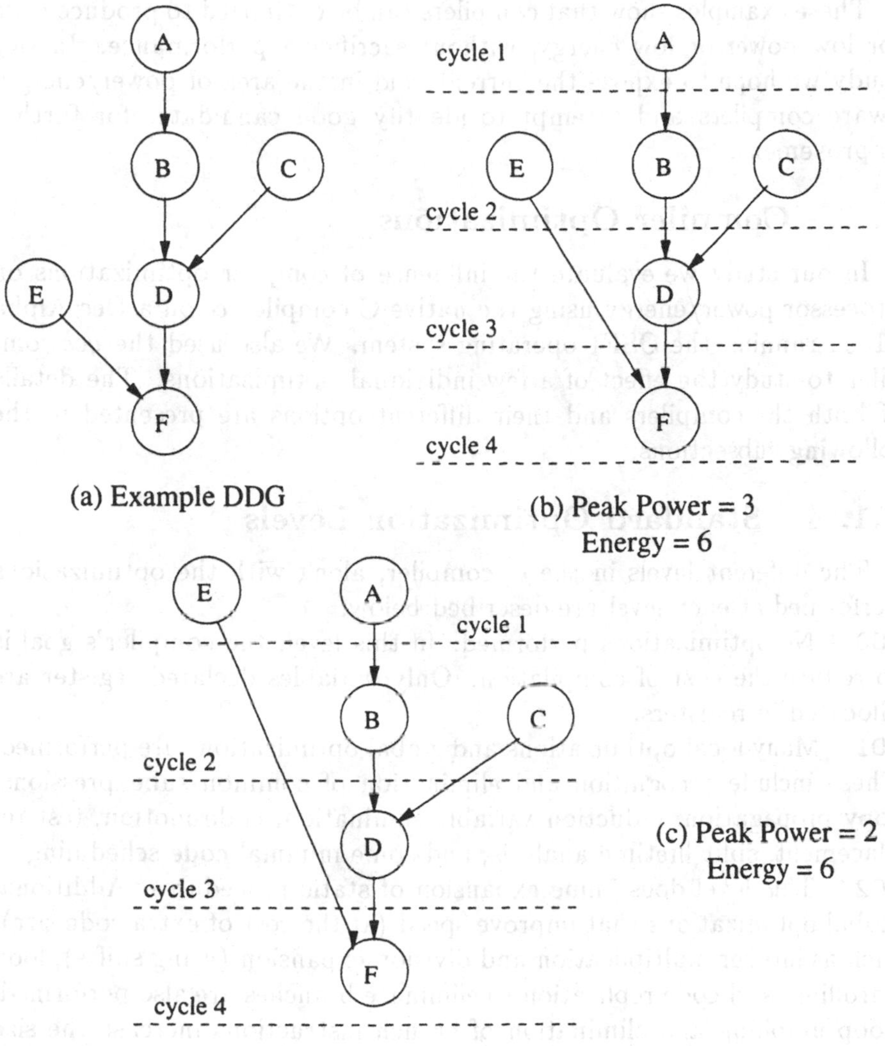

Figure 6.1. Motivating Example

Another good candidate for reducing energy without increasing power would be function-in-lining. Function-in-lining is done in cases where the callee procedure body is small. In these cases, the code required for the calling sequences outweigh the code in the procedure body. If this procedure is called many times, in-lining can save a tremendous number of instructions. Function-in-lining does not increase the overlap such as instruction scheduling, hence this optimization keeps energy low and holds the power constant. This optimization can be a good candidate to use in the "compile for power/energy" switch.

These examples show that compilers can be optimized to produce code for low power or low energy, without sacrificing performance. In this study we hope to expose the current void in the area of power/energy-aware compilers and attempt to identify good candidates for further improvement.

4. Compiler Optimizations

In our study we evaluate the influence of compiler optimizations on processor power/energy using the native C compiler *cc* on a Dec Alpha 21064 running the OSF1 operating system. We also used the *gcc* compiler to study the effect of a few individual optimizations. The details of both the compilers and their different options are presented in the following subsections.

4.1. Standard Optimization Levels

The different levels in the *cc* compiler, along with the optimizations performed at each level are described below.

`-O0` No optimizations performed. In this level, the compiler's goal is to reduce the cost of compilation. Only variables declared register are allocated in registers.

`-O1` Many local optimizations and global optimizations are performed. These include recognition and elimination of common subexpressions, copy propagation, induction variable elimination, code motion, test replacement, split lifetime analysis, and some minimal code scheduling.

`-O2` This level does inline expansion of static procedures. Additional global optimizations that improve speed (at the cost of extra code size), such as integer multiplication and division expansion (using shifts), loop unrolling, and code replication to eliminate branches are also performed. Loop unrolling and elimination of branch instructions increase the size of the basic blocks. This helps the hardware exploit instruction level parallelism (ILP) in the program.

`-O3` Includes all `-O2` optimizations and also does inline expansion of global procedures performed.

`-O4` Software pipelining, an aggressive instruction scheduling technique used to exploit ILP in loops is performed using dependency analysis. Vectorization of some loops on 8-bit and 16-bit data is also done. This level also invokes a scheduling pass which inserts NOP instructions to improve the scheduling.

We use the FORTRAN *g77* compiler to compile the SpecFP benchmarks. *g77* is a program to call *gcc* with options to recognize programs written in Fortran. The standard optimization levels offered by *gcc* are listed below:

`-O0` No optimizations performed.

`-O1` This level is very similar to the `-O1` in *cc*. Optimizations performed are common subexpression elimination, combining instructions through substitution (copy propagation), dead-store elimination, loop strength reduction and minimal scheduling.

`-O2` Nearly all supported optimizations that do not involve a space-speed tradeoff are performed. Loop unrolling and function inlining are not done, for example. This level also includes an aggressive instruction scheduling pass.

`-O3` This turns on everything that `-O2` does, along with also inlining of procedures.

We note that in both *cc* and *gcc*, the optimizations that increase the ILP in a program are in optimization levels `-O2`, `-O3` and `-O4` (`-O4` only in *cc*). The different levels include almost the same optimizations in both the compilers. We use both *cc* and *gcc* in our work. We use *cc* wherever possible, and *gcc* wherever specific hooks to control individual optimizations are required.

4.2. Individual Optimizations

We analyze the impact of four different individual optimizations provided by *gcc*. We chose *gcc* for this because *gcc* provides more number of distinct individual optimizations than *cc* to chose from. All the individual optimizations are applied on top of optimizations performed at `-O1`. The individual optimizations chosen are:

-fschedule-insns This optimization attempts to reorder instructions to eliminate execution stalls that occur due to unavailability of required data. This helps machines that have slow floating point or memory load instructions by allowing other instructions to be issued until the result of the load or floating point instruction is required. The scheduler used is a basic-block list-scheduler and it is run after local register allocation has been performed.

-fschedule-insns2 Similar to *-fschedule-insns*, but requests an additional pass of instruction scheduling after register allocation has been done. This pass does aggressive global scheduling before and after global register allocation. Postpass scheduling (when scheduling is done after register allocation) minimizes the pipeline stalls due to the spill instructions introduced by register allocation.

-finline-functions Integrates all simple functions into their callers. The compiler heuristically decides which functions are simple enough to be worth integrating in this way.
-funroll-loops Perform the optimization of loop unrolling. This is done only for loops whose number of iterations can be determined at compile time or run time.

5. Experimental Results

In this section we first describe the Wattch simulator and our benchmarks. We then present a detailed analysis of our results.

5.1. Wattch 1.0 and Benchmarks

We use the Wattch 1.0 simulator [2] for our experimentation. Wattch is an architectural simulator that estimates CPU energy consumption. The power/energy estimates are based on a suite of parameterizable power models for various hardware structures in the processor and on the resource usage counts. The power models are interfaced with *Simplescalar* [4]. `sim-outorder`, *Simplescalar's* out-of-order issue simulator has been modified to keep track of which unit is being accessed in each cycle and record the total energy consumed for an application.

Wattch has three different options for clock gating to disable unused resources in the processor. The simplest clocking style assumes that the full modeled power will be consumed if any accesses occur in a given cycle, and zero otherwise. This is ideal clock gating. The second possibility assumes that if only a portion of a unit's port are accessed, the power is scaled linearly according to the number of ports being used. In the third clock gating scheme, power is scaled linearly with port or unit usage, but unused units dissipate 10% of their maximum power. This corresponds to the static power dissipated when there is no activity in unit. We chose power and energy results corresponding to the third scheme since it is the most realistic of all schemes. We used the default configuration in `sim-outorder` for our study, but changed the RUU (Register Update Unit) from 16 to 32 and LSQ (Load Store Queue) size from 8 to 16. The functional unit latencies exactly match the functional units latencies in the Alpha 21064 processor. We use the process parameters for a .35um process at 600MHz.

We chose six different benchmarks for our study - three SpecInt95 benchmarks, namely *compress, go* and *li*, two SpecFp95 benchmarks *su2cor* and *swim*, and *saxpy*, a toy benchmark.

5.2. Results

In the following subsections we present a detailed analysis of the results obtained. We first discuss the influence of standard optimizations on energy and power following which we study the affects of individual optimizations.

5.2.1 Influence of Standard Optimizations on Energy.

Table 6.1 shows the results obtained when the benchmarks are compiled with different standard optimizations levels. We present the results of all optimizations relative to the result of optimization level -O0. For example, when we consider the number of instructions, the percentage of instructions executed by a benchmark optimized with option -O2 is given by:

$$\% \text{ of Insts Executed by } Prog_{O2} = \frac{\# \text{ of Insts Executed by } Prog_{O2}}{\# \text{ of Insts Executed by } Prog_{O0}} * 100$$

For example, in Table 6.1, we see that *compress* when compiled with -O2 executed 17.96% fewer instructions than *compress* when compiled with -O0. Our results are presented in this form for all benchmarks and for all optimizations. As mentioned in Section 4, we used *cc* to compile the SpecInt benchmarks and *saxpy* and *g77* to compile the SpecFP benchmarks *su2cor* and *swim*.

We observe that the number of instructions committed drops drastically from optimization -O0 to -O1, and also drops significantly in codes optimized with -O2 and -O3. There is however a very marginal increase in the number of instructions in *compress.* In codes optimized with -O4 option, the number of instructions increases due to the extra NOPs code generated for scheduling.

The reduction in number of instructions directly influences execution time or performance. The performance improvement is significant in -O1 when compared to -O0, sometimes as high as 73% (*swim*). -O2, -O3 also lead to significant improvement over -O1, for example, we see an 8% improvement in *li* with -O2 optimization. In some benchmarks like *saxpy* the improvement is only about 0.6%. Optimizations -O2, -O3 improve performance in *compress* even though the number of instructions increases.

The energy consumed by the code is again directly proportional to the number of instructions. Here we see that even though -O2 and -O3 improve performance in *compress*, the energy consumed is higher. This is because of the higher number of instructions. Hence, the amount of work done is more. In all the benchmarks, we see that the energy decreases when the number of instructions decrease. Hence, if we are

Table 6.1. Effects of Standard Optimization on Power/Energy

Benchmark	opt level	Energy	Exec Time	Insts	Avg Power	IPC
compress	O0	100.00	100.00	100.00	100.00	100.00
	O1	74.48	81.55	81.52	91.33	99.96
	O2	75.13	81.44	82.04	92.25	100.73
	O3	75.13	81.44	82.04	92.25	100.73
	O4	79.01	82.77	86.11	95.45	104.03
go	O0	100.00	100.00	100.00	100.00	100.00
	O1	66.20	64.13	68.94	103.23	107.50
	O2	62.62	61.31	63.01	102.14	102.78
	O3	62.62	61.31	63.01	102.14	102.78
	O4	63.67	62.19	63.75	102.38	102.51
li	O0	100.00	100.00	100.00	100.00	100.00
	O1	81.32	83.66	83.18	97.20	99.42
	O2	79.60	75.97	82.97	104.78	109.21
	O3	79.60	75.97	82.97	104.78	109.21
	O4	85.71	77.89	90.96	110.05	116.78
saxpy	O0	100.00	100.00	100.00	100.00	100.00
	O1	97.38	100.24	92.49	97.15	92.27
	O2	97.69	99.38	92.49	98.30	93.07
	O3	97.69	99.38	92.49	98.30	93.07
	O4	98.31	99.27	92.84	99.02	93.51
su2cor	O0	100.00	100.00	100.00	100.00	100.00
	O1	42.09	51.04	33.21	82.46	65.06
	O2	40.99	47.52	33.10	86.28	69.67
	O3	40.99	46.37	33.10	87.65	71.38
swim	O0	100.00	100.00	100.00	100.00	100.00
	O1	30.10	36.64	20.01	82.15	54.63
	O2	28.93	34.01	19.05	85.06	56.01
	O3	28.93	34.01	19.05	85.06	56.01

compiling for energy, we should chose optimizations such as common sub-expression elimination, induction variable elimination and unrolling that reduce the number of instructions executed. Optimizations such as the ones in -O4 (inserting NOPs to improve scheduling), may improve performance, but can also increase the number of instructions, leading to higher energy requirements. The energy increase is seen to be up to 4% (in *compress*).

5.2.2 Influence of Standard Optimizations on Power. To study the influence of compiler optimizations on power, we again refer to Table 6.1. We see that though the number of instructions and the number of cycles taken reduces in higher optimization levels, the number of instructions do not reduce enough to keep the instructions per cycle (IPC) constant. IPC reduces in `-O1` codes but increases in `-O2`, `-O3` and `-O4` codes. IPC in `-O0` is low because of the poor quality of code produced. Since optimizations such as common subexpression elimination improve code by reducing instructions rather than increasing available parallelism, IPC does not increase in `-O1` codes. Most optimizations that increase IPC such as instruction scheduling, loop unrolling etc are included in `-O2`, `-O3` and `-O4` levels. Power dissipated is the amount of work done in one cycle. This is directly proportional to the IPC. Hence, we see that optimizations that increase IPC, increase the power dissipated. Instruction scheduling and other `-O2`, `-O3` optimizations are good for performance improvement but are bad when instantaneous power is the main concern.

5.2.3 Influence of Individual Optimizations on Energy and Power. We refer to Tables 6.2 to 6.7 for experiments on how the different individual optimizations effect power/energy. We show the results for each benchmark separately. The tables show the performance, power and energy of each of the optimizations relative to performance, power and energy of code with `-O0` (similar to Table 6.1). Since the individual optimizations are applied over the `-O1` option, in our discussions, we always compare results of the optimizations with results of `-O1`. We first discuss the effects of the instruction scheduling options.

Table 6.2. Individual Optimizations on Compress

opt level	Energy	Exec Time	Insts	Power	IPC
O0	100.0	100.0	100.0	100.0	100.0
O1	67.66	74.68	60.46	90.60	80.95
inline-func	67.69	74.68	60.46	90.63	80.95
sched-instr2	68.82	74.94	63.21	91.82	84.35
sched-instr	66.66	73.47	59.83	90.72	81.43
unroll-loops	66.84	74.19	59.90	90.09	80.74

The *-fschedule-instr* optimization does simple basic block list-scheduling and *-fschedule-instr2* does aggressive global scheduling. We expect both options to increase the IPC and hence the power. We can see from the tables that IPC goes up in most benchmarks, in some benchmarks up to 4.6% (in *su2cor*). The power increase is up to 3.9% . In *li*, the power increases by as much as 10%. The aggressive scheduler (prepass scheduler) increases register pressure and hence causes significant number of spills, thereby increasing the total number of instructions executed and the to-

Table 6.3. Individual Optimizations on li

opt level	Energy	Exec Time	Insts	Power	IPC
O0	100.00	100.00	100.00	100.00	100.00
O1	70.91	74.67	66.18	94.96	88.63
inline-func	71.02	73.14	68.00	97.11	92.97
sched-instr2	69.56	66.65	68.33	104.36	102.52
sched-instr	69.56	66.65	68.33	104.36	102.52
unroll-loops	66.05	59.91	68.19	110.24	113.81

Table 6.4. Individual Optimizations on saxpy

opt level	Energy	Exec Time	Insts	Power	IPC
O0	100.00	100.00	100.00	100.00	100.00
O1	96.78	98.56	96.21	98.19	97.61
inline-func	96.78	98.56	96.21	98.19	97.61
sched-instr2	97.07	97.14	96.27	99.93	99.11
sched-instr	96.79	98.52	96.15	98.24	97.60
unroll-loops	96.87	98.72	95.97	98.13	97.21

Table 6.5. Individual Optimizations on su2cor

opt level	Energy	Exec Time	Insts	Power	IPC
O0	100.00	100.00	100.00	100.00	100.00
O1	42.09	51.04	33.21	82.47	65.07
inline-func	42.06	51.01	33.21	82.46	65.11
sched-instr2	42.49	50.36	34.02	84.38	67.55
sched-instr	40.90	47.79	33.30	85.58	69.67
unroll-loops	40.17	48.35	31.17	83.08	64.46

tal energy. The increase in number of instructions and energy are up to 3.52% and 2.14% respectively. This optimization needs to be improved upon if power and energy are a concern. We would see a greater impact of these optimizations if the target processor was an in-order machine, wherein the compiler is fully responsible for exposing the parallelism. In an out-of-order issue machine, the hardware can find the parallelism even if the compiler does not do any reordering. The reason why we see some improvement in performance (and increase in IPC) is because the hardware is limited by the instruction window size, the global scheduler

Table 6.6. Individual Optimizations on swim

opt level	Energy	Exec Time	Insts	Power	IPC
O0	100.00	100.00	100.00	100.00	100.00
O1	30.06	36.64	20.02	82.02	54.64
inline-func	30.06	36.64	20.02	82.02	54.64
sched-instr2	30.91	36.39	20.53	84.92	56.41
sched-instr	29.83	35.11	20.32	84.95	57.86
unroll-loops	29.29	35.38	18.19	82.80	51.43

Table 6.7. Individual Optimizations on go

opt level	Energy	Exec Time	Insts	Power	IPC
O0	100.00	100.00	100.00	100.00	100.00
O1	40.97	42.75	42.65	95.83	99.77
inline-func	40.92	42.78	42.58	95.64	99.54
sched-instr2	43.07	44.01	45.25	97.87	102.82
sched-instr	43.52	44.89	46.52	96.96	103.63
unroll-loops	39.38	41.95	39.30	93.88	93.69

which has the full program as its scope helps the hardware see more instructions than it otherwise would have.

We next discuss the impact of unrolling. Unrolling appears to be a good optimization to use for energy because the number of instructions reduce significantly. We are able to reduce the number of instructions by 3.35% in *go*, the energy falls by 1%. We see that in the some benchmarks the energy falls by 5% (*li*). However, reducing the energy does not necessarily reduce power. For instance, in *li*, the power goes up by 10%. Unrolling increases the size of the basic block, hence allows the hardware increase the overlap of instructions. This leads to an increase in the number of simultaneous operations being executed. It may be noted that the IPC in *li* increases by 25%. However, this observation is not consistent among all the benchmarks, in many benchmarks, there is no increase in IPC. This is because the target architecture has a good branch predictor, it does unrolling in hardware, hence reducing the impact of software unrolling. We are currently investigating how the unrolling optimization affects power if we turned off the branch prediction hardware. We expect to see a significant increase in IPC and power in the codes after unrolling has been applied.

Our next optimization is inlining of function calls. Inlining as explained in the motivation section will reduce the number of instructions and hence energy. However, in our benchmarks, only *go* and *su2cor* show a very marginal decrease in energy. In our future work, we will be investigating further with a better set of benchmarks more suited for this optimization.

6. Conclusions

In this chapter we evaluated the impact of using the different levels of optimizations in the *cc* compiler on system power and energy. We also evaluated the effect of a few individual optimizations. We found that the energy consumption reduces when the optimizations reduce the number of instructions executed by the program, i.e., when the amount of work done is less. The standard optimization level `-O1` reduces the number of instructions drastically as compared to `-O0` because it invokes optimizations such as common subexpression elimination, an optimization used to eliminate redundant computations in the program. The drop is not that significant in `-O2, -O3 and -O4` optimizations. The energy also drops in the same proportion.

We found power dissipation to be directly proportional to the average IPC of program. `-O2, -O3 and -O4` levels have significantly higher IPC and hence higher average power. The optimization levels `-O2, -O3 and -O4` include optimizations such as instruction scheduling, which are typically used to increase the parallelism in the code.

Out of the four individual optimizations we evaluated, we found unrolling to be a good optimization for energy reduction but it increases power dissipation. Function inlining is good for both energy reduction and reducing power dissipation. Instruction scheduling was found to be a bad optimization to use when power is a concern. Simple schedulers did not affect the energy consumption, but aggressive schedulers i.e., schedulers that increased register pressure and introduced spills, increased the energy consumption as well. For our future work, we would like to evaluate more individual optimizations and improve the ones that we find are currently unoptimized for power or energy.

References

[1] Asanovic, K. (2000). Energy-exposed instruction set architectures. In *Work In Progress Session, Sixth International Symposium on High Performance Computer Architecture*.

[2] Brooks, D., Tiwari, V., and Martonosi, M. (2000). Wattch: A framework for architectural-level power analysis and optimizations. In

27th International Symposium on Computer Architecture.

[3] Bunda, J., Athas, W. C., and Fussell, D. (1994). Evaluating power implication of cmos microprocessor design decisions. In *1994 International Workshop on Low Power Design.*

[4] Burger, D. and Austin, T. M. (1997). Evaluating future microprocessors: The simplescalar tool set. Technical report, Dep. of Comp. Sci., Univ. of Wisconsin, Madison.

[5] Gowan, M. K., Biro, L. L., and Jackson, D. B. (1998). Power considerations in the design of the alpha 21264 microprocessor. In *Design Automation Conference*, pages 726–731.

[6] Hajj, N. B. I., Polychronopoulos, C., and Stamoulis, G. (1998). Architectural and compiler support for energy reduction in the memory hierarchy of high performance microprocessors. In *ISLPED 98*, pages 70–75.

[7] Kandemir, M., Vijaykrishnan, N., Irwin, M. J., and Ye, W. (2000). Influence of compiler optimizations on system power. In *Design Automation Conference.*

[8] Kin, J., Gupta, M., and Mangione-Smith, W. H. (1997). The filter cache: An energy efficient memory structure. In *30th International Symposium on Microarchitecture*, pages 184–193.

[9] Manne, S., Klauser, A., and Grunwald, D. (1998). Pipeline gating: Speculation control for energy reduction. In *25th International Symposium on Computer Architecture*, pages 1–10.

[10] Su, C.-L. and Despain, A. M. (1995). Cache designs for energy efficiency. In *28th Annual Hawaii International Conference on System Sciences*, pages 306–315.

[11] Su, C. L., Tsui, C. Y., and Despain, A. M. (1994). Low power architecture design and compilation techniques for high-performance processors. In *IEEE COMPCON.*

[12] Toburen, M. C., Conte, T. M., and Reilly, M. (1998). Instruction scheduling for low power dissipation in high performance microprocessors. In *Power-Driven Microarchitecture Workshop In Conjunction With ISCA 1998.*

Chapter 7

A TECHNOLOGY-SCALABLE ARCHITECTURE FOR FAST CLOCKS AND HIGH ILP

Karthikeyan Sankaralingam
Computer Architecture and Technology Laboratory
Department of Computer Sciences
The University of Texas at Austin
karu@cs.utexas.edu

Ramadass Nagarajan
Computer Architecture and Technology Laboratory
Department of Computer Sciences
The University of Texas at Austin
ramdas@cs.utexas.edu

Doug Burger
Computer Architecture and Technology Laboratory
Department of Computer Sciences
The University of Texas at Austin
dburger@cs.utexas.edu

Stephen W. Keckler
Computer Architecture and Technology Laboratory
Department of Computer Sciences
The University of Texas at Austin
skeckler@cs.utexas.edu

Abstract CMOS technology scaling poses challenges in designing dynamically scheduled cores that can sustain both high instruction-level parallelism and aggressive clock frequencies. In this paper, we present a new architecture that maps compiler-scheduled blocks onto a two-dimensional grid of ALUs. For the mapped window of execution, instructions execute in a dataflow-like manner, with each ALU forwarding its result along short wires to the consumers of the result. We describe our studies of program behavior and a preliminary evaluation that show that this architecture has the potential for both high clock speeds and high ILP, and may offer the best of both the VLIW and dynamic superscalar architectures.

Keywords: Static scheduling, dynamic issue, dataflow, instruction level parallelism, VLIW, out-of-order execution.

1. Introduction

Conventional microarchitectures have been improving in performance by approximately 50-60% per year, improving the instructions per cycle (IPC) using more transistors on a chip and increasing the clock speed. However both strategies will fail for future technologies (50nm and below), with clock speed growth slowing down because of fundamental pipelining limits and wire delays making architectures communication bound [1]. Thus, today's architectures will not scale, showing diminishing returns in IPC even with increasing chip transistor budgets. New designs must address these issues, efficiently utilizing the increasing transistor budget while overcoming communication bottlenecks.

One approach for extracting ILP is through conventional superscalar cores that detect parallelism at run-time. The amount of ILP that can be detected is limited by the issue window, whose logic complexity grows as the square of the number of entries [12]. Conventional architectures also rely on many frequently accessed global structures, such as register files, re-order buffers and issue windows, which become bottlenecks limiting clock speed or pipeline depths.

Another approach for extracting parallelism is taken by VLIW machines, in which ILP analysis is performed at compile time. Instruction scheduling is performed by the compiler, orchestrating the flow of execution statically. This approach performs well only for regular workloads and suffers from the drawback that dynamic events are not handled well — a stall in one functional unit forces the entire machine to stall, since all functional units must be synchronized.

In this paper, we describe a new architecture called the Grid Processor that takes into consideration the technology constraints of wire delays and pipelining limits. The compiler is used to detect parallelism and statically schedule instructions on a computation substrate, but instructions are issued dynamically. We propose an execution substrate that consists of a set of *named distributed computing elements* to which the compiler statically assigns individual instructions.

The architecture does not suffer from VLIW issue restrictions, as instructions are issued dynamically and executed in a dataflow fashion. Instructions from a compiler-generated basic block or hyperblock are mapped statically to nodes in the computation array, with each node being assigned one or more instructions. The nodes issue instructions dynamically when the input operands are available. Temporary values produced and consumed inside a block are not visible to the architectural state, and are instead forwarded directly from the producers to their consumers.

We propose a fine-grained partitioning of the issue window and associated functional units (FU). The computation array includes both a grid of issue window-FU pairs (nodes) and a dedicated communication network for passing data. Data produced at a node are routed dynamically through intermediate nodes to their eventual destinations. The architecture is a hybrid between conventional superscalar and conventional VLIW architectures, issuing instructions dynamically with

In the Grid Processor, the available transistor budget is used to build an array of computation elements aimed at overcoming several challenges of communication overhead in future systems. First, by forwarding values directly between producers and consumers, the reliance on centralized structures is reduced. Second, compiler controlled physical layout ensures that the critical path is scheduled along the shortest physical path. Finally, instruction blocks are mapped onto the grid as single units of computation amortizing scheduling and decode overhead over a large number of instructions. The reduced reliance on centralized structures allows the computation substrate to be clocked at high speeds.

The remainder of this paper is organized as follows. Section 2 describes the key features of the Grid Processor and demonstrates how programs are mapped onto it. Section 3 characterizes certain aspects of program behavior indicating that existing applications are amenable for execution on the Grid Processor. Section 4 describes related work pertaining to wide-issue and dataflow oriented machines. Section 5 concludes with a discussion on some of the secondary advantages including power reduction and speculation control as well as the remaining issues to be solved.

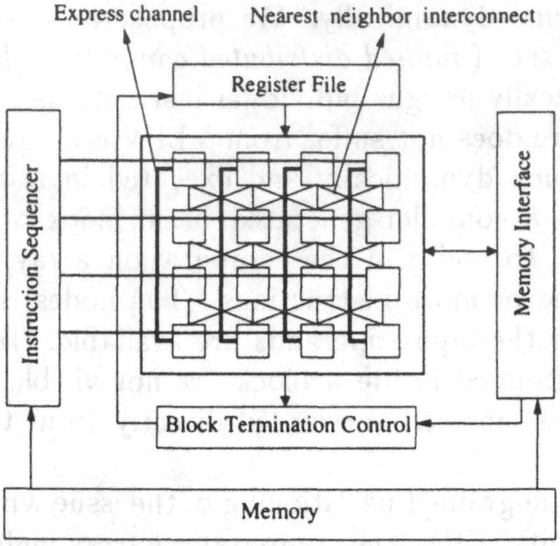

Figure 7.1. Grid block diagram. Express channels connect the last row with the first row

2. Architecture

The Grid Processor consists of a computation substrate that is configured as a two-dimensional grid of fine-grained computation nodes connected by an interconnection network. The compiler partitions the program into a sequence of blocks (basic blocks or hyperblocks [16]), performs renaming of temporaries, and schedules instructions in a block to nodes of the grid. Instruction traces generated at run-time could be used instead of blocks generated by the compiler. Blocks are fetched one at a time and their instructions are mapped to the computation nodes *en masse* as assigned by the compiler. Execution proceeds in a dataflow fashion with each instruction sending its results directly to other instructions that use them. A set of interfaces are used by the computation substrate to access external data.

2.1. Computation Nodes

Figure 7.1 shows a high level overview of the grid with some of the associated interfaces. Nearby neighbors in the grid are connected by short wires that have small communication delays [1]. Fast express channels connect nodes that are physically far apart in the grid. The instruction sequencer fetches blocks of instructions from the instruction memory and

[1] The figure shows one possible grid interconnect topology as an example only.

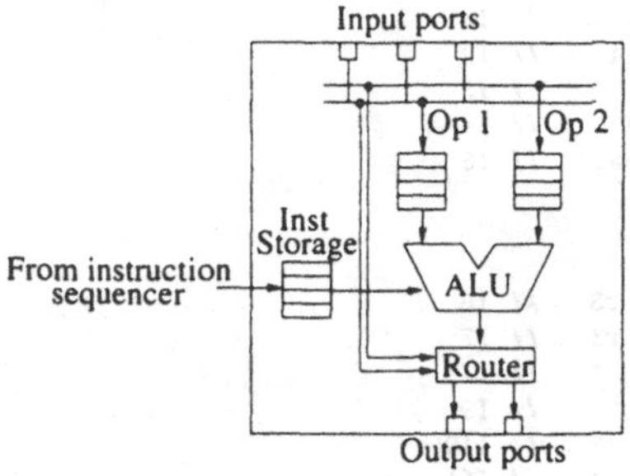

Figure 7.2. Organization of a computation node

places those instructions on the nodes as scheduled by the compiler. The block termination control interfaces with the register file and the memory interface, detects when a block completes execution, and commits architecturally visible data to the register file and memory. The memory interface is used to communicate with the load/store queue, caches, and main memory.

The computation nodes are lightweight units that perform the function of execution, temporary storage, and data forwarding. Each computation node consists of a set of functional units, storage structures, an instruction wakeup unit, a router, and read/write ports for communication. Figure 7.2 shows the layout of a computation node. The functional units consist of an integer unit and optionally a floating point unit that perform the actual execution. The storage structures include a set of queues and buffers for storing the instructions, their input operands, and data tokens that need to be forwarded to other nodes in the grid. The instruction wakeup unit matches instructions with their operands as they arrive and issues them to the functional units for execution. The router examines tokens in the storage structures and forwards them along one of the many paths out of this node to their eventual targets. Data tokens meant for other nodes bypass the ALU and are directly forwarded by the router to their destinations.

2.2. Execution Model

The compiler partitions the program into a sequence of *blocks.* Blocks are constructed such that there are no internal control flow changes, and all control transfers out of a block initiate instructions in other blocks. These blocks may be basic blocks, hyperblocks, or program traces generated at run-time. Figure 7.3 shows a stream of instructions that has been partitioned by the compiler into three different blocks (basic blocks in this case) B1, B2, and B3. Explicit *move* instructions, separate from the

```
0x0000 add r1, r2, r3     // I1
0x0004 add r2, r2, r1     // I2
0x0008 ld r4, (r1)        // I3
0x000c add r5, r4, 1      // I4
0x0010 beqz r5, 0xdeac    // I5

// End of block B1

0x0014 add r10, r2, r3    // I6
0x0018 add r11, r2, r3    // I7
0x001c ld r4, (r10)       // I8
0x0020 ld r5, (r11)       // I9
0x0024 mul r31, r4, r5    // I10
0x0028 bne r31, 0xbee0    // I11

// End of block B2

0x002c xor r8, r5, 1      // I12
0x0030 sll r9, r4, r8     // I13
0x0034 add r13, r9, 8     // I14
0x0038 add r12, r9, r2    // I15
0x004c sw r13, r12        // I16

// End of block B3

0x0050 add r1, r6, r9
....
0x0070 jmp 0x0050
```

Figure 7.3. A sample instruction stream

computation instructions, are generated for the registers read by every block. The move instructions fetch block inputs from the register file and pass them as internal (temporary) values to the block. Figure 7.4 shows the Data Flow Graph (DFG) of the blocks B1, B2, and B3 in Figure 7.3 along with the *move* instructions. As shown in the figure, all instructions have been renamed with temporary registers for their operands and *move* instructions generated for every input register. For example, in block B1, two move instructions, `move t2,r2` and `move t3,r3` are generated by the compiler for input registers r2 and r3. Inside a block, all values are referenced using temporary names. The *move* instructions associates register inputs of the block and temporaries. Data values that must be passed to other blocks are written to the register file.

At run-time, the instruction sequencer fetches a block from the instruction memory and maps it onto the grid *en masse*; there is no serialization of fetch, decode and rename for the instructions within a block. Individual instructions are written to the storage structures of the nodes to which they have been assigned at compile time. Block execution is initiated by the move instructions which read register data and send them to their consumers. The instruction wakeup unit matches incoming data with an instruction and issues ready instructions to the functional unit

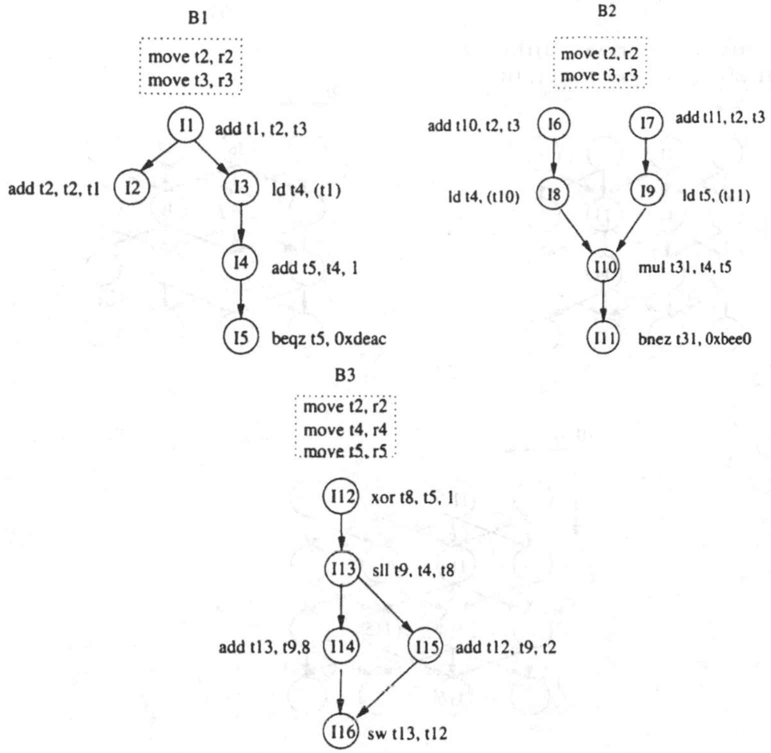

Figure 7.4. Basic blocks shown as dataflow graphs. Registers are marked with "r" and temporaries with "t".

for execution. The results of the computation are tagged and forwarded by the router through the interconnect to their eventual destinations.

2.2.1 Instruction Mapping. The compiler generates a mapping by physically laying out the data flow graph of each block on a grid. Every computation instruction in the block is assigned to a node in the grid, with the critical path scheduled along the shortest possible physical path. All output operands are renamed with the positions of consumer nodes. Move instructions serve the purpose of associating register data with positions of their consumer nodes. Figure 7.5 illustrates a layout of the grid with instructions mapped on the computation elements. Instructions I1 and I2 of block B1 in Figure 7.4 are mapped on the grid at positions (0,1) and (1,1) respectively. Correspondingly, the move instruction `move t2, r2` has (0,1) and (1,1) encoded in its destination fields and register name r2 in its input field.

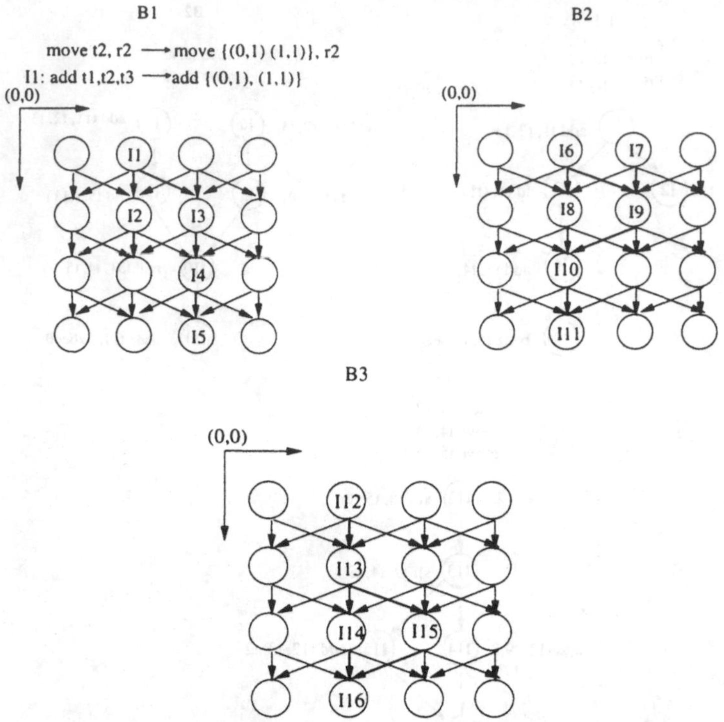

Figure 7.5. Basic blocks mapped on a grid of dimension 4x4, with the 3 nearest neighbors reachable directly. Instruction destinations are ordered pairs (x, y), which identify a consumer with a relative position x nodes below and y nodes to the right of the producer.

2.2.2 Instruction Wakeup and Execution. As described in section 2.1, multiple instructions are mapped onto a single node and data are written to an operand buffer when they arrive. Upon arrival of a data token, the instruction and operand buffers are examined to wake-up and issue ready instructions. The wakeup delays will be considerably smaller than seen in conventional cores because of smaller issue windows. The computation node serially performs two operations whenever an operand arrives — *wakeup* and *execute*. Serializing wakeup and execute may increase the cycle time along the execute-execute path of dependent instructions. Wakeup-execute can be pipelined into two stages, if the instruction wakeup does slow the clock. The execute phase of the producer can be overlapped with the wakeup phase of its consumer.

Conventional superscalar cores have dedicated bypass paths to forward data which can be used to guarantee that following the execution of an instruction its dependents will have that data in the next cycle.

In the Grid Processor, since data are routed dynamically, there is no dedicated path that is guaranteed to be free when an instruction completes execution to forward its data to its consumer. However, there are several mechanisms that can alleviate this problem. Special wakeup tokens could be generated during the issue stage of a producer instruction. They reach the consumer nodes at the end of the stage, reserving a channel for the data to follow in the next cycle. Alternately, speculative instruction issue could be used to hide the select latency with local rollback mechanisms in the event of incorrect issue.

2.2.3 Block Mapping. The instruction and operand storage structures at a node can be used to buffer multiple instructions and data, which are associated through tags. There are three reasons to have multiple instructions mapped on a node. First, graphs larger than the physical grid can be folded over and mapped on the grid with more than one instruction at a node. Second, instructions from different blocks that are fetched speculatively (using control speculation or from speculative threads [19]) can be mapped at a node. Finally, blocks from different threads can also be mapped to support multithreading.

2.3. Instruction Encoding

The Grid Processor ISA is divided into data movement instructions and computation instructions. Data movement instructions include *move*, *split* and *repeat* instructions. The *move* instructions fetch block inputs from the register file and pass them as temporary values to the block. Encoding space limitations restrict the number of targets that can be specified in an instruction. The *split* instructions replicate data to reach additional targets. The range of each target (distance from the producer) that can be specified is finite. The *repeat* instructions are used to forward data to targets outside the range. There is a trade-off between the instruction size, number of specifiable targets and the range of each target.

Every instruction is encoded with an opcode field, destination field, and in the case of *move* instructions, an input field. The destination field consists of multiple targets, with each target encoded with the position of the consumer expressed as an offset. The *move* instructions are encoded with an input register name and its destinations. Figure 7.5 shows a sample encoding of a move instruction and a computation instruction. The *move* instruction `move t2,r2` is encoded as `move (0,1),(1,1),r2` corresponding to the input register r2 and consumer instructions I1 and I2 that are mapped at (0,1) and (1,1) respectively. Instruction I1 is encoded with destinations corresponding to consumers I2 and I3 of the temporary t1. I2 is mapped at the node directly below I1 and I3 is mapped at the node one to the right and one below I1. An extra bit (not shown in the figure) is necessary to specify the order of the input operands.

2.4. Role of the Compiler

The compiler plays an important role in the Grid Processor. Apart from detecting ILP, the compiler constructs blocks that are scheduled on the grid, and defines mechanisms for intra and inter-block communication. The compiler must also generate data movement instructions to overcome encoding space limitations.

In the Grid Processor, blocks are fetched as a single unit, mapped on the grid, and executed in a dataflow fashion. Since the instructions are fetched at a block granularity, it is desirable to have large blocks and good *block utilization.* Block utilization is defined as the ratio of dynamically executed instructions to the static size of the block. One method of building large blocks is to build hyperblocks based on profiling information. Register file communication for data passed between successively executed blocks can be bypassed using the grid interconnect, thereby "stitching" these blocks as a single dataflow graph. The compiler must define interfaces and mechanisms to stitch together multiple blocks. Since data movement instructions add overhead, when scheduling the graph, the compiler should minimize the critical path and attempt to minimize the number of such instructions.

3. Preliminary Analysis

In this section, we investigate the amenability of existing applications to the Grid Processor and examine few aspects of program behavior that affect performance. Large blocks with a significant number of block temporaries and a few input and output registers are desirable because they have low register file bandwidth. It is also desirable to have large blocks with high utilization to amortize the cost of block fetch and map. The encoding space needed for representing temporaries is determined by the number of targets of an instruction. Fewer average targets per value produced permits a compact encoding. We examine these characteristics in existing applications to determine how well they map onto the Grid Processor.

In our experimental analysis, SPEC CPU2000 benchmarks were compiled using the Trimaran [20] tool set. Three floating point *(equake, ammp and art)* and three integer *(parser, gzip and mcf)* benchmarks were selected for analysis. Hyperblocks were generated for these bench-

Benchmark	Average Instructions per block			
	Static Size	Dynamically Executed	Never executed due to early branches	NOPs
gzip	144	77	59	8
mcf	48	35	8	5
parser	29	27	1	1
art	129	125	2	2
equake	57	52	2	3
ammp	124	103	8	13

Table 7.1. Block utilization

marks using Trimaran's IMPACT compiler with the *train* input set for profiling. All of the benchmarks were simulated using the Trimaran simulator for 500 million instructions with the *ref* input set. We collected dynamic statistics using modifications made to the simulator to track block size profiles and register usage.

3.1. Instruction Behavior

In this section, we examine some aspects of program behavior. Performance is affected by the block sizes in programs and grid configurations. A profile of the dynamic block size was obtained for all the benchmarks to analyze the trade-off of block size with respect to block utilization. Wide grids have better performance at the cost of increased area with fewer nodes having mapped instructions. We analyze this trade-off for three different grid widths.

3.1.1 Block Size. From our analysis of the SPEC CPU2000 benchmarks, we observed that large hyperblocks can be built. Figure 7.6 shows the dynamic block size profiles for the different benchmarks. For each of the benchmarks, the figure plots the percentage of execution time spent for each dynamic block size as a cumulative distribution function. Dynamic block size is the number of instructions in a block that are actually executed, excluding predicated instructions that are converted to NOPs.

Nearly 70% of the execution time is spent in blocks of size greater than 26 for the integer benchmarks and blocks of size greater than 65 for the floating point benchmarks. Across the benchmarks, the average number of dynamic instructions in a block ranges from 27 to 125.

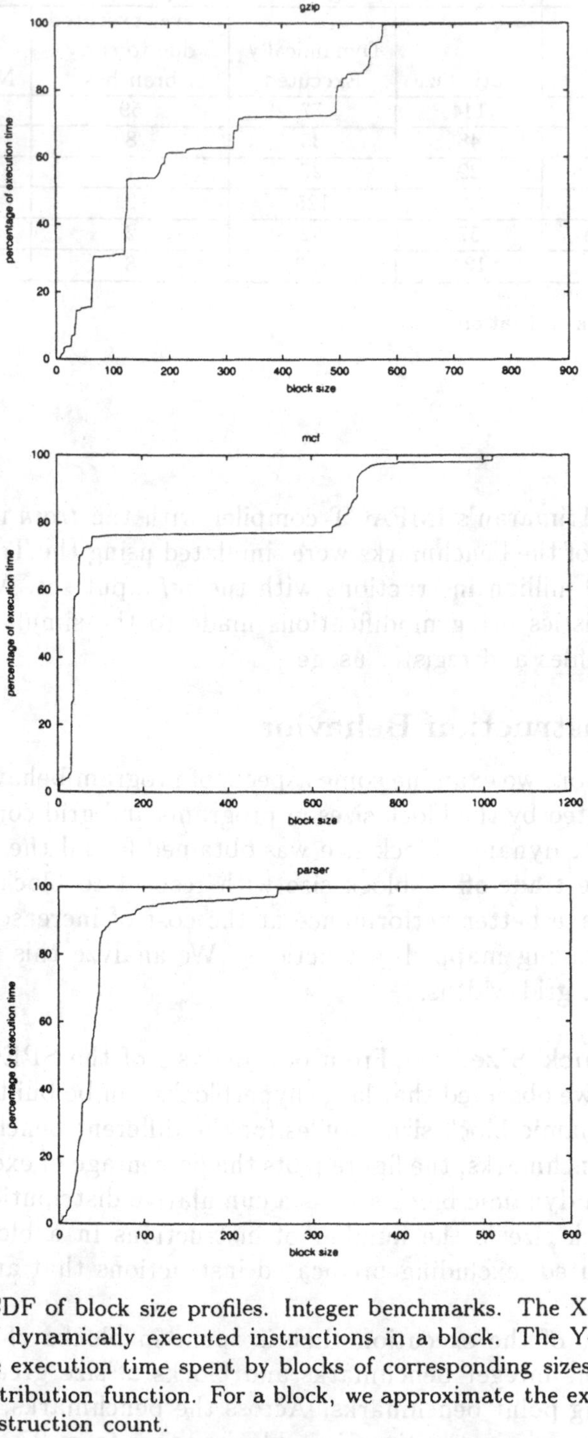

Figure 7.6. CDF of block size profiles. Integer benchmarks. The X-axis represents the number of dynamically executed instructions in a block. The Y-axis represents the percentage execution time spent by blocks of corresponding sizes expressed as a cumulative distribution function. For a block, we approximate the execution time as its dynamic instruction count.

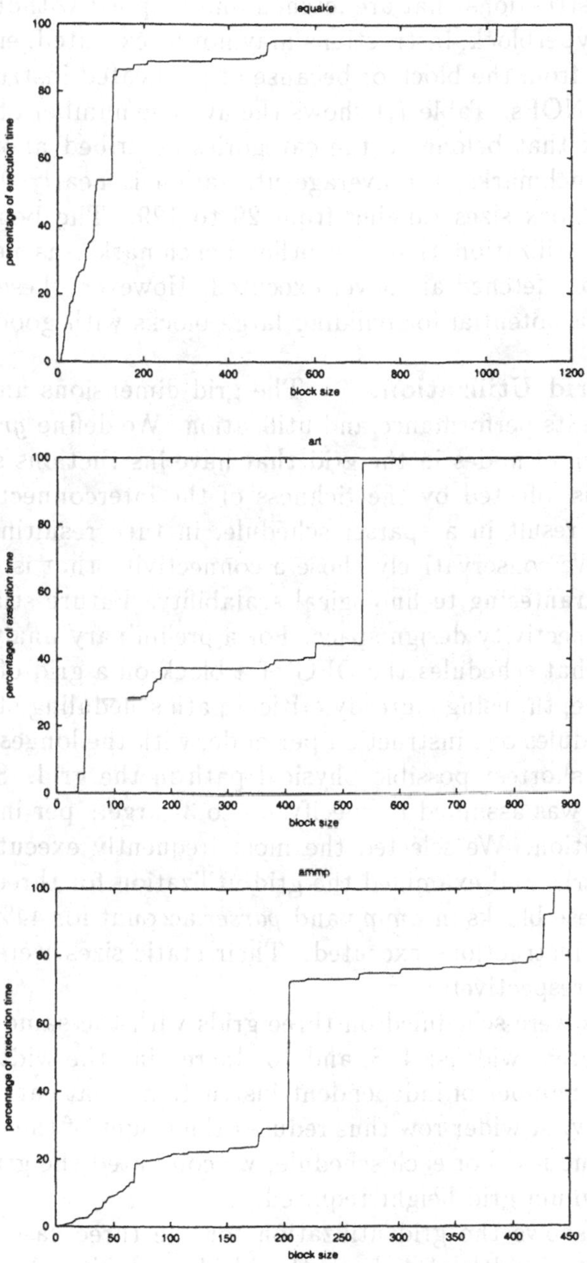

Figure 7.6 (continued). FP benchmarks

High utilization percentages are desirable because blocks are fetched and mapped as a single unit. Blocks with poor utilization have a large number of instructions that are fetched and mapped without being executed. In a hyperblock, instructions may not be executed, either because of early exits from the block or because of predicated instructions being converted to NOPs. Table 7.1 shows the average number of instructions in each block that belong to the categories described above. For four of the six benchmarks, the average utilization is nearly 90% with average static block sizes ranging from 29 to 129. The benchmark *gzip* shows worse utilization than the other benchmarks, as nearly 40% of the instructions fetched are never executed. However, these preliminary results show a potential for building large blocks with good utilization.

3.1.2 Grid Utilization. The grid dimensions and connectivity determine its performance and utilization. We define *grid utilization* as the fraction of nodes in the grid that have instructions scheduled on them. This is affected by the richness of the interconnect: fewer connections will result in a sparser schedule, in turn resulting in a lower utilization. We conservatively chose a connectivity that is relatively restrictive, guaranteeing technological scalability. Future studies will explore the connectivity design space. For a preliminary analysis, we used a simulator that schedules the DFG of a block on a grid of finite width and infinite depth, using a greedy critical path scheduling strategy. This strategy schedules one instruction per node, with the longest path in the DFG on the shortest possible physical path in the grid. Sufficient encoding space was assumed to specify up to 3 targets per instruction, at any grid position. We selected the most frequently executed blocks in two benchmarks and examined the grid utilization for three grid configurations. These blocks in *ammp* and *parser* account for 44% and 15% of the dynamic instructions executed. Their static sizes were 218 and 43 instructions, respectively.

The blocks were scheduled on three grids with the same connectivity of 3, but different widths: 4, 8, and 16. Increasing the width of the grid increases the number of independent instructions that can be scheduled in a single row. A wider row thus reduces the height of the schedule, but wastes more nodes. For each schedule, we computed the grid utilization and the minimum grid height required.

Table 7.2 shows the grid utilization for the three cases. The table shows that at a width of 4, both the blocks exhibit a high utilization of 99% and 83%, requiring a grid height of 55 and 13 respectively. An increase in the grid width to 8 decreases the height by 8 in *ammp* and 4 in *parser*, improving performance but with poorer node utilization. As

Width	Min. height	Nodes	Utilization
ammp — 218 insts			
4	55	220	99%
8	43	344	63%
16	39	624	35%
parser — 43 insts			
4	13	52	83%
8	9	72	72%
16	7	112	46%

Table 7.2. Grid utilization for different grid widths, for the most frequently executed blocks in *ammp* and *parser*.

the width is further increased to 16, the drop in the height is less, but the utilization drops dramatically. The best balance of the grid height and node utilization is at 8. We note that mapping multiple blocks from same or different threads may increase the utilization at a minimal cost.

3.2. Register Behavior

Block inputs and block outputs are data read from and written to the register file. The number of such inputs and outputs determine the bandwidth and number of ports required at the register file. Block temporaries are data created and used within a block. With a large number of temporaries, a significant amount of communication through the register file can be eliminated. We report the results of our simulations to estimate the number of input registers, output registers and block temporaries used during program execution.

3.2.1 Input, Output and Temporary Data. In a "well-behaved" block, the number of register inputs and outputs is small and the number of temporaries large. Table 7.3 shows the number of input, output and temporaries used on the six selected benchmarks. The percentage of executed blocks versus the number of registers for the three different types is shown. For example, in the benchmark *ammp*, fewer than 5 registers are written out by 94.6% of the blocks executed, and an additional 4.2% of the blocks output between 5 and 9 registers.

The integer and FP benchmarks show slightly different behavior. More than 75% of the blocks in the integer benchmarks read or write fewer than 10 registers. For the FP benchmarks, more than 75% of the blocks read or write less than 20 registers. The larger number is due to the larger block sizes for the FP benchmarks, for which the average

Number of regs	% of blocks ammp	equake	art	gzip	parser	mcf
Input registers						
0-4	88.6	32.1	1.0	48.2	82.9	93.5
5-9	5.2	32.9	0.3	34.8	15.2	2.9
10-14	4.4	19.5	19.8	11.6	1.0	1.3
15-19	0.5	1.5	56.8	5.0	0.4	2.2
>= 20	0.4	13.5	22.0	0.0	0.3	0.0
Temporary registers						
0-9	39.8	47.4	20.6	37.6	85.8	32.9
10-19	14.9	16.6	38.1	19.1	3.5	3.1
20-29	5.1	10.3	18.8	18.4	10.0	59.6
30-39	13.0	1.7	0.0	0.4	0.2	2.9
40-49	1.3	4.5	0.8	14.3	0.0	0.0
50-59	0.8	0.3	0.0	0.0	0.0	0.0
60-69	2.3	5.4	1.6	0.5	0.0	7.1
70-79	0.0	0.0	3.6	2.2	0.0	0.0
80-89	0.0	0.0	0.6	0.5	0.0	0.0
90-99	22.3	1.0	0.5	0.1	0.0	0.0
>= 100	0.0	11.0	0.0	0.3	0.0	7.1
Output registers						
0-4	94.6	63.4	20.1	62.9	97.6	97.6
5-9	4.2	6.4	0.8	15.0	2.0	1.9
10-14	0.2	21.8	37.8	18.5	0.2	0.4
15-19	0.9	6.8	25.6	3.3	0.0	0.1
>= 20	0.0	1.2	15.6	0.0	0.0	0.0

Table 7.3. Input, Output and Temporary registers used by the blocks.

block size is almost twice that of the integer benchmarks. Except for *parser*, all of the benchmarks have at least 10 temporaries in over 50% of the blocks, showing that a significant reduction in register bandwidth can be achieved by the internal renaming provided in this architecture.

3.2.2 Register fanout. Limited instruction encoding space constrains the number of consumers that can be specified. *Fanout* refers to the number of targets for which an instruction can produce data. Large-fanout instructions require extra *split* instructions to reach all consumers. Figure 7.7 shows the average fanout for each produced value in the various benchmarks. For all 6 benchmarks, the fanout is 1 for more than 60% of instructions and less than or equal to 2 for more than 80% of the instructions. This shows that, if we support at least two targets, only one-fifth of the producers require *split* instructions.

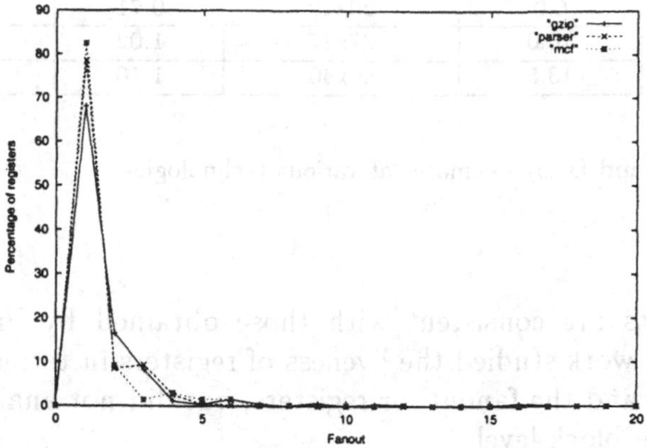

Figure 7.7. Register fanout — Number of targets for each produced value. Integer benchmarks

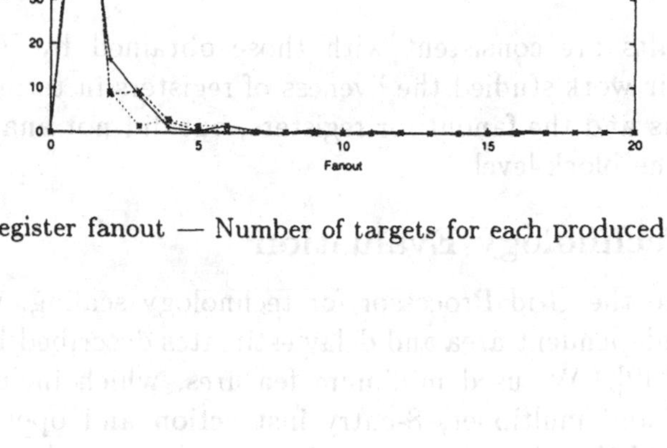

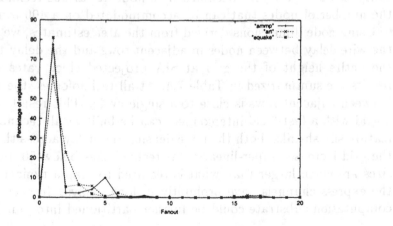

Figure 7.7 (continued). FP benchmarks

Technology (nm)	Clock Speed (GHz)	Grid Dimensions in 400 mm^2	Row Delay (cycles)	Grid Height Delay (cycles)
100	3.5	10x10	0.53	3.57
70	6.0	20x20	0.71	5.83
50	10.0	27x27	1.02	11.02
35	13.5	40x40	1.16	21.30

Table 7.4. Area and Delay estimates at various technologies

These results are consistent with those obtained by Franklin and Sohi [8]. Their work studied the liveness of registers in terms of number of instructions and the fanout for registers, but did not analyze register behavior at the block level.

3.3. Technology Evaluation

To evaluate the Grid Processor for technology scaling, we used the technology-independent area and delay estimates described by Gupta [9] and Agarwal [2]. We used minimum features, which include a 64-bit integer ALU and multiplier, 8-entry instruction and operand buffers, and an 8-bit ALU and buffers for the router at each node. We assumed that 50% of the chip area is reserved for the grid interconnect. We computed both the area occupied by a node at various technologies and the number of nodes that can be accommodated on a 400 mm^2 chip.

Using node dimensions derived from the area estimates, we computed the wire delay between nodes in adjacent rows and the delay to traverse the entire height of the grid at SIA projected clock rates [17]. The results are summarized in Table 7.4. At all technologies, the wire delay between adjacent rows is close to a single cycle. This result shows that a grid with a fast local interconnect can be built at all technologies. As feature size shrinks, both the node density and delay across the height of the grid increases super-linearly. At technologies below 50 nm, the grid sizes are much larger than what is required to map a typical block and the express channels have prohibitively long delays. In such cases, the computation substrate could be further partitioned into multiple grids.

4. Related Work

There have been a number of related approaches preceding the Grid Processor. Dennis and Misunas proposed a static dataflow architecture with programs expressed in a Fortran-like dataflow language [6].

Arvind proposed the Tagged-Token Dataflow architecture with purely data-driven instruction scheduling for programs expressed in a dataflow language [3]. Culler proposed a hybrid dataflow execution model where programs are partitioned into code blocks made up of instruction sequences called threads with dataflow execution between threads [5]. Our approach uses a conventional programming interface with dataflow execution for a limited window of instructions.

We take a hybrid approach between VLIW [7] and conventional superscalar architectures by statically scheduling the instructions using the compiler and dynamically issuing them. There have been other efforts to enhance dynamic execution in VLIW machines. Rau proposed a split-issue mechanism to separate register read and execute from writeback and a delay buffer to support dynamic scheduling for VLIW processors [14].

Others have looked at various naming mechanisms for values to reduce the register pressure and register file size. Smelyanskiy proposed Register Queues for allocating live values in software pipelined loops [18]. Llosa proposed register sacks, which are low bandwidth port-limited register files for allocating live values in pipelined loops [11]. Corporaal proposed an explicitly specified communication mechanism in Transport Triggered Architectures for general purpose computing [4].

Many researchers are exploring distributed or partitioned uniprocessor designs. Waingold proposed a distributed execution model with extensive compiler support in the RAW architecture [21]. The RAW architecture assumes a coarser-grain execution than does the Grid Processor, exploiting parallelism across multiple compiler-generated instruction streams. Ranganathan and Franklin described an empirical study of decentralized ILP execution models [13]. Sohi proposed Multiscalar processors where a single program is broken up into a collections of tasks. The tasks are distributed to a number of parallel processing units which reside within a processor complex [19]. Each of these units fetches and executes instructions belonging to its assigned task. Rotenberg proposed trace processors where several processing elements work on different traces of the program, passing data values using a common register bus [15]. Unlike the trace processor, the Grid Processor executes a trace in a fine-grain dataflow fashion and overlaps multiple traces on the same computation substrate.

Finally, Patt proposed a Block-Structured Instruction Set Architecture for increasing the fetch rate for wide issue machines where the atomic unit of execution is a block and not an instruction [10].

5. Conclusion

In this paper, we have proposed a technology-driven architecture that combines the advantages of compiler-scheduled instruction level parallelism with data-driven execution on a fast clocked grid of execution units. Instruction blocks are mapped onto the grid as single units of computation, amortizing the fetch and decode over a large number of instructions. Access to global storage elements such as register files is reduced by maintaining temporaries as transient values within the grid. Overheads can further be reduced by overlapping the execution of one instruction block with the fetch and mapping of the next.

Our initial evaluation indicates that existing programs are ripe to be mapped to this substrate. Typical block sizes range from 27 to 125 dynamically executed instructions, which we anticipate to be sufficiently large to amortize scheduling overheads. The number of input and output values required for a large fraction of the blocks is less than 10 in five of the six benchmarks, indicating that the amount of register file communication between blocks is small. The average number of temporary registers per block is larger, ranging from 10 to 30, depending on the benchmark. This range indicates that a substantial amount of communication to the centralized register file can be eliminated through the producer/consumer communication within the grid. Finally, the average number of consumers of a produced value is only 1.9, which shows that the network within the grid does not require large bandwidth for intra-block communication.

In addition to these direct performance advantages, the proposed Grid Processor provides several other benefits. It offers substantial power savings because much of the scheduling is performed at compile time and each execution unit is idle until all operands arrive. Furthermore, since particular blocks of the program, such as loops, can be mapped once and reused many times, the time and power required for block mapping can be reduced substantially. In conventional architectures, the instructions must be fetched repeatedly for each iteration of the loop. This *mapping reuse* may permit the Grid Processor to act as a high performance substrate for DSP codes as well. Finally, the data driven computation model on the Grid Processor is amenable to both polypath execution and selective re-execution upon mis-speculation. Conditionally executed instructions within the block can be started speculatively. If the speculation was incorrect, the block may be re-executed by loading correct values into the appropriate graph nodes and letting the values propagate to the data dependent downstream instructions. Thus no instructions need be refetched, and independent instructions do not need to be re-executed upon a mis-speculation rollback.

While this paper outlines the basic Grid Processor architecture and its potential for performance improvement, substantial challenges lie ahead in the complete design. The dataflow-style execution is amenable to both computation and memory parallelism. However, dynamic dependences between loads and stores must be detected to ensure proper ordering in the memory system. Dynamic dataflow execution with compiler-controlled static scheduling removes the need for synchronization in the execution substrate that conventional architectures enforce. The challenge lies in detecting when all of the instructions in the block have terminated and architecturally visible storage can be committed. Finally, the traditional precise exception model in which an exception can occur at any point in the instruction stream is particularly challenging for the Grid Processor. Changing the granularity of rollback from an instruction to a block level may enable more efficient exception implementation.

Acknowledgements

Many thanks to the anonymous reviewers and the CART group members for their feedback on early versions of this paper. This work is supported by the National Science Foundation under CAREER awards CCR-9985109 and CCR-9984336, CISE Research Instrumentation grant EIA-9985991, University Partnership Awards from IBM, and a grant from the Intel Research Council.

References

[1] V. Agarwal, M. S. Hrishikesh, S. W. Keckler, and D. Burger. Clock rate versus IPC: The end of the road for conventional microarchitectures. In *Proceedings of the 27th Annual International Symposium on Computer Architecture*, pages 248–259, June 2000.

[2] V. Agarwal, S. W. Keckler, and D. Burger. Scaling of microarchitectural structures in future process technologies. Technical Report TR2000-02, Department of Computer Sciences, The University of Texas at Austin, Austin, TX, February 2000.

[3] Arvind and R. S. Nikhil. Executing a program on the MIT Tagged-Token Dataflow Architecture. *IEEE Transactions on Computers*, 39(3):300–318, 1990.

[4] H. Corporaal. *Transport Triggered Architectures.* PhD thesis, Delft University of Technology, September 1995.

[5] D. E. Culler, A. Sah, K. E. Schauser, T. von Eicken, and J. Wawrzynek. Fine-grain parallelism with minimal hardware support: A compiler-controlled threaded abstract machine. In *"Proceedings of the 4th International Conference on Architectural Support for Programming Languages and Operating Systems*, pages 164–175, April 1991.

[6] J. Dennis and D. Misunas. A preliminary architecture for a basic data-flow processor. In *Proceedings of the 2nd Annual Symposium on Computer Architecture*, pages 126–132, January 1975.

[7] J. Fisher. Very long instruction word architectures and the ELI-512. In *Proceedings of the Tenth Annual International Symposium on Computer Architecture*, pages 140–150, June 1983.

[8] M. Franklin and G. Sohi. Register traffic analysis for streamlining inter-operation communication in fine grain parallel processors. In *Proceedings of the 25th Annual International Symposium on Microarchitecture*, pages 236–245, 1992.

[9] S. Gupta, S. W. Keckler, and D. Burger. Technology independent area and delay estimates for microprocessors building blocks. Technical Report TR2000-01, Department of Computer Sciences, The University of Texas at Austin, Austin, TX, February 2000.

[10] E. Hao, P. Chang, M. Evers, and Y. Patt. Increasing the instruction fetch rate via block-structured instruction set architectures. In *Proceedings of the 29th International Symposium on Microarchitecture*, pages 191–200, December 1996.

[11] J. Llosa, M. Valero, J. Fortes, and E. Ayguade. Using sacks to organize register files in VLIW machines. In *CONPAR 94 - VAPP VI*, September 1994.

[12] S. Palacharla, N. P. Jouppi, and J. E. Smith. Complexity-effective superscalar processors. In *Proceedings of the 24th Annual International Symposium on Computer Architecture*, pages 206–218, June 1997.

[13] N. Ranganathan and M. Franklin. An empirical study of decentralized ILP execution models. In *8th International Conference on Architectural Support for Programming Languages and Operating Systems*, pages 272–281, October 1998.

[14] B. Rau. Dynamically scheduled VLIW processors. In *Proceedings of the 26th Annual International Symposium on Microarchitecture*, pages 80–90, December 1993.

[15] E. Rotenberg, Q. Jacobson, Y. Sazeides, and J. Smith. Trace processors. In *Proceedings of the 30th Annual International Symposium on Microarchitecture*, pages 138–148, December 1997.

[16] S.A.Mahlke, D.C.Lin, W.Y.Chen, R.E.Hank, and R.A.Bringmann. Effective compiler support for predicated execution using the hyperblock. In *Proceedings of the 25th Annual International Symposium on Microarchitecture*, pages 45–54, June 1992.

[17] The national technology roadmap for semiconductors. Semiconductor Industry Association, 1999.

[18] M. Smelyanskiy, G. Tyson, and E. Davidson. Register queues: A new hardware/software approach to efficient software pipelining. In *International Conference on Parallel Architectures and Compilation Techniques (PACT 2000)*, October 2000.

[19] G. Sohi, S. Breach, and T. Vijaykumar. Multiscalar processors. In *Proceedings of the 22nd International Symposium on Computer Architecture*, pages 414–425, June 1995.

[20] Trimaran : An infrastructure for research in instruction-level parallelism. http://www.trimaran.org.

[21] E. Waingold, M. Taylor, D. Srikrishna, V. Sarkar, W. Lee, V. Lee, J. Kim, M. Frank, P. Finch, R. Barua, J. Babb, S. Amarsinghe, and A. Agarwal. Baring it all to software: RAW machines. *IEEE Computer*, pages 86–93, September 1997.

Topic Index

Author Index